FINDING
Freedom
from FEAR

David Wright

FINDING *freedom* from FEAR

A Contemporary Study from the Psalms

Lamplighter Books Grand Rapids, Michigan
Zondervan Publishing House

FINDING FREEDOM FROM FEAR
Copyright © 1990 by David Wright

Lamplighter Books are published by Zondervan Publishing House
1415 Lake Drive, S.E., Grand Rapids, MI 49506

Library of Congress Cataloging-in-Publication Data

Wright, David (David W.)
   Finding freedom from fear / David Wright.
     p. cm.
   "Lamplighter books."
   ISBN 0-310-44351-2
   1. Fear—Religious aspects—Christianity. 2. Christian
life—1960– 3. Wright, David (David W.) I. Title.
BV4908.5.W75 1989
248.8′6—dc20   89–28604
                                                                       CIP

All Scripture quotations, unless otherwise noted, are taken from the *Holy
Bible: New International Version* (North American Edition). Copyright ©
1973, 1978, 1984 by the International Bible Society. Used by permission of
Zondervan Bible Publishers.

Edited by Carol Uridil, John Sloan
Designed by Louise Bauer

Printed in the United States of America

90 91 92 93 94 95 / LP / 10 9 8 7 6 5 4 3 2 1

For Helen, Christin, and Annie

CONTENTS

PREFACE

Some days life seems bent on convincing us that "To be human is to be in danger." Threatening circumstances, events, and people crowd in from all sides.

Fear and anxiety affect all of us. Not one of us makes it through life without facing private nightmares. The massive horrors this century has provided are our daily companions. Any realistic view of life must see it as complex, ambiguous, often delightful, but also potentially horrible.

We often face a compound problem. We live a highly pressured existence in which global threats never seem to abate and personal failure seems disastrous. Fear is a natural consequence of that kind of life. But our society considers fear shameful and unacceptable.

Our most-used greeting is, "How are you?" The expected response is, "Fine, thank you," delivered in a convincing tone, with a bright smile.

We have little space in our lives for people who aren't well, who are unable to cope with life's circumstances. We push them aside, shut them up in brightly lit, antiseptic rooms—closing them from our minds and our fellowship.

This makes fear and anxiety worse. Not only must we face the threats of life, but we must carry on as though we haven't a care. For many, this burden becomes unbearable.

They turn to compulsive behavior, violence, and self-destruction. They lose perspective, courage, and hope.

The scientific study of this problem has blossomed into an enormous field. Researchers and therapists continue to develop and apply various theories. The field is approached in three ways.

One approach tries to find and treat the physiological elements of fear and anxiety. What chemical and neurological processes take place when a person feels anxiety? Great strides have been made in this research. (As a result, doctors are able to prescribe some drugs to treat chemical and hormonal causes of fear.)

The second approach has followed the revolutionary work of Sigmund Freud by attempting to search out the sources and mechanisms of fear hidden deep within the human psyche. Many of the therapists use psychoanalytic techniques pioneered by this approach.

A third approach, based on cognitive theory, has developed more recently. Rather than focusing primarily on the physiological elements of fear, or on its affective and behavioral aspects, cognitive therapists study the way people take in and use mental information. They focus on the way we think about ourselves and the world.

All of us interpret the events and circumstances of our lives differently. Researchers have found these interpretations result in automatic thoughts and mental images about daily events. They have found that when we are in the grip of problem anxieties, these mental images and automatic thoughts are unrealistic and catastrophic.

Cognitive therapies aim to help us examine and modify ourselves and our world. They provide practical mental tools to deal with anxiety.

In this study I have relied heavily on concepts drawn from the cognitive approach.[1] This does not mean I am attempting to force the Bible truths and the experiences of believers into a foreign mold. Cognitive therapists have discovered the importance of, and are working to help people work with, issues the Bible addresses.

In his long history with humankind, God has sought to help us deal with our self-concept and our mental approach toward life. God has always invited us to be his children, to face life from a context of holiness, praise, and community. He gives us his grace and asks for our faithfulness. We have the long history of his care, his ceaseless love, his constant presence. These truths are tremendous resources to help us orient our lives and to find confidence in the face of fear.

We need not be ashamed of our fear. Best of all, we need not be overcome with fear. God in his great grace reaches out to fold us into himself. While this does not insure us against danger—we still must live in this world— it does give us resources upon which to draw to find freedom from fear.

This study represents a personal journey taken through the twists and turns of my heart. I now see myself in new ways. I have renewed appreciation for the joys of my walk with God.

I look forward to sharing these ideas with fellow believers.

NOTES

[1]An abundance of literature is available to those who would like to learn more about cognitive therapy. A good starting place is the book by Dr. Aaron T. Beck, Dr. Gary Emery, and Ruth L. Greenberg entitled *Anxiety Disorders and Phobias: A Cognitive Perspective* (New York: Basic Books, 1985). I have made use of several ideas found in that book.

ACKNOWLEDGMENTS

The task of writing a book is complex, sometimes laborious, but always rewarding. The reward I treasure most is the opportunity to minister to the body of Christ.

A seminary professor once used the story of Jesus and the woman at the well of Samaria to illustrate the fulfillment we find in doing the will of God. After Jesus had his conversation with the woman, his disciples asked if he had eaten. Jesus replied, "My food . . . is to do the will of him who sent me." (John 4:34).

The joy of doing what God has called me to do gives me something like the pleasure and nourishment of daily meals.

There are other rewards. I've learned much about fear. I've learned about myself. I've met many interesting and helpful people both face-to-face and through their writing. I have had the privilege of taking on a task bigger than myself and seeing the heavenly Father assist me in bringing it to completion. Best of all I've caught new glimpses of the glory, breadth, and depth of life in Christ.

I'd like to thank several people whose generous help made this book possible. Dr. Wayne Caldwell and Mrs. Alberta Metz read early drafts of the manuscript and offered constructive criticism. This project would never have been attempted without the godly example of my parents. Their consistent godly witness has taught me much about the spiritual resources available in our walk with God.

My mother, Mrs. Virginia Wright, gave her considerable talents to preparing the study guides for each chapter.

I also thank two editors whose expertise and guidance helped make this book possible. Ms. Janet Kobobel, though she did not work on this manuscript, was an invaluable help at a crucial period in my life. Mr. John Sloan urged me to develop this study from my experiences in Haiti, then did all the tedious tasks good editors do to bring books to life.

Finally I would like to thank my wife and daughters for their patience and love, not only during the hectic months of working on this manuscript but through the many days of the adventure we shared. Helen listened to ideas, read drafts of chapters, and provided encouragement. She gives me the priceless asset of an ear tuned to the practical realities of life. My daughters, Christin and Annie, make my world a place where I daily learn the meanings of love and delight.

David Wright
Lexington, Kentucky

1
THE DAILY ADVENTURE
OF LIVING
WITH CONFIDENCE

I will never forget the evening when violence broke out in our town of Petit Goave, Haiti. We had finished supper. A small errand took me outside. I walked onto our back porch, then down the path under the big mango trees in our backyard.

Suddenly a dull roar rolled down from the highway a quarter mile away. As I turned to listen, gunshots rang out. The roar of the crowd rose. The gunfire increased.

My three-year-old daughter had followed me down the path. She stared at me, eyes wide with astonishment. Scooping her up, I ran back to the house. My wife and a missionary couple met me at the door.

"It's started," I said. "Keep the girls inside. I don't know how far away the gunfire is. They may come this way." I ran outside to watch and listen.

That evening we sat and listened to the gunfire and the crowd. After several hours the crowd was quieted and driven into hiding. The rest of the night, patrols of fully-armed soldiers roamed the streets.

As missionaries working in Haiti, we watched the political tension and social turmoil grow as the people became more dissatisfied with the political regime. Friends and neighbors often talked to us fearfully. Their furtive glances and hushed tones revealed a fear that every word could be used against them. Students demonstrated. Violence splattered fresh blood on the desolate Haitian soil. Our town, along with many others, became a focus of unrest. We wondered how long it would be before a full-fledged civil war broke out.

As tensions increased, roads were often closed. Since travel was restricted, food became difficult to keep on hand. We worried for our own safety, but our hearts ached for Haitian friends and co-workers who watched as their country fell apart. Almost every day brought new stories of people killed around the country.

Fear was no stranger before the events of those tumultuous days. Like any normal person I had faced my share of threatening circumstances before, both imagined and real. Some fears were private and intense, known only to me and the few I confided in. Other fears were trivial and easily dismissed.

I began to learn the scope of fear's devastating power during those days of turmoil in Haiti. It came to disrupt life and drain my spiritual strength. Fear clouded my judgment and made decisions difficult. Worst of all, the relationship with God that had always been a source of strength and comfort now seemed empty and useless.

Suddenly fear was no longer just a nuisance. It demanded answers that too often escaped me.

These experiences brought me to a crisis. My walk with God, the equilibrium of my life, was put to new tests.

As I've wrestled with the problem of fear, I've come to see how widespread it is among believers. I believe the need to find freedom from fear is one of the most important personal issues facing contemporary Christians.

Some of my experiences have been unique. But the problem I'm addressing is not. You have fears hidden away in your mind, just as I have. One perplexing aspect of this problem is that following Christ doesn't exempt us from fear.

Sometimes, usually in novels, we read about someone's fear vanishing. Fears do come and go. But if they vanish it can only be because we've dealt with their sources and found confidence to go on in peace despite threatening circumstances.

The question at the heart of this book is this: What unique spiritual resources do Christians have with which to face and conquer fear?

This book will not toss out a few platitudes to assure us that life in this fallen world can be free of fear. Neither is this a psychological treatise that can substitute for counseling and professional care for those suffering from extreme anxiety disorders.

I believe that one of our greatest joys is to discover and use the spiritual resources that are our heritage as believers. In them we have sources of strength to face fear, worry, and anxiety.

So what can you expect to find in this book? Here's how we'll approach the topic.

We cannot conquer fear until we begin to understand it. That's our first task. We won't attempt to reproduce all the perspectives and arguments written about fear. Instead we'll discuss a simple way of thinking about fear that helps in dealing with it.

Our next task will be to lay out a basic approach for coping with fear. We will outline a simple plan explaining how to cope with anxiety.

The plan is simple. This doesn't mean the process of overcoming anxiety is easy. Anxiety can be a powerful opponent. But this plan will help. It is found (in different forms) in various therapeutic approaches. By using it, we can begin dealing constructively with anxiety.

We get to the heart of our study after completing the previous two tasks. What unique resources does our walk with God offer to help us deal with anxiety? To answer that, we'll rely on the richest mine of personal spiritual reflection in the Bible—the Psalms. We find a wealth of insight into the spiritual resources available for coping with fear by studying David's spiritual life.

I don't think of these spiritual resources as psychological techniques or therapeutic methods. They are not cure-alls that guarantee freedom from anxiety. Instead, they are reservoirs from which we can draw new perspective, courage, and hope. With them we can face anxiety, accept it as a part of life, and do the work needed to conquer it.

As we begin this study, you must know I still face fear. If you're looking for someone who can give tidy answers or offer a way to live free of all fear, this probably isn't the book for you. But come along if you'd like to share in an honest inquiry into the sources of strength that are ours in Christ.

Living with confidence is a daily adventure. The God of eternity lives as hope in my heart. The strength of his grace and glory brings courage. Yes, fear can sometimes fill my life with shadows, but as I capture the light of eternity in my soul I find I can pass through the darkness of this world shining.

The study of fear is a positive adventure; the circum-stances that call forth fear provide the chance to discover ourselves. Fear strips us of pretense, of our cultivated public images.

The great blessing of fear, when we can see it, is that it shows us ourselves as we really are. We can use fear as an occasion to face spiritual realities, to dig deeply into truth until our faith in Christ is warmhearted and true. The power of a living relationship with God does not exempt us from fear but gives us courage to conquer fear.

I invite you along on this daily adventure. Our goal is to learn to conquer the fears that plague us, and to stand together as examples of our Father's grace in this world.

2

UNDERSTANDING OUR BUILT-IN ALARM

You know what fear feels like. Your hands get clammy. Your stomach tightens. Your breath comes in short gasps. Your body tenses. Suddenly, everything but your fear fades into the background—your attention is riveted on whatever has triggered it. You can't think straight. For an instant you may forget familiar things, even your own name.

A wave of terrible emotion controls you. Stark, painful images may come into your mind. You feel vulnerable, doomed. When the fear subsides, you feel utterly exhausted.

When I was learning to become a pilot the mixture of emotions was almost indescribable. While driving to the airport, I would feel great excitement. I loved flying. But then I would start thinking of all that could go wrong, remembering all the mistakes I could make. The consequences of a serious error in flying would flood my mind.

Then a small but insistent voice would hound me. "You can't do this. Who do you think you are? Sure, you did okay last time, but do you really think you'll never make a fatal error? Come on. Better quit. Better play it safe."

If I didn't overcome my fear two results were possible. My ability to fly safely would be impaired, or I would give up flying altogether.

The circumstances may be different for you. Perhaps some aspect of your job seems beyond your capacity. You can't even think about it without breaking out in a sweat. Perhaps you feel threatened by a certain person. Having to face that person ties you in knots.

Or, you may feel a vague anxiety that refuses to go away. You can't say exactly what causes it, but the feeling is real. It drains your energy, leaves you irritable, and makes life a chore.

The task is to discover the comfort and courage our relationship with Christ provides for conquering all kinds of fear. Before doing that, here are some important points to consider.

What Does It Mean to Conquer Fear?

First we must understand what it means to fear.

We will never find any magical ways to guarantee ourselves a life without fear. The only way to do that would be to step outside of life—to retreat into death, the world of chemical dependencies, or some other unreal world.

When I refer to conquering or finding freedom from fear, I don't mean we can escape from the possibility of fear.

Think of the example of David in the Bible. He was a heroic figure, but he was also very real. What makes him so appealing is that the Bible doesn't cover up the vulnerable side of his life.

David faced many fearful circumstances. His fear often came from the threats of personal enemies. Sometimes it came from remorse about his own failures. Other times his fear came from life circumstances that seemed out of control. David knew all about fear. But what kind of person do we find reflected in the psalms? Was David timid, withdrawn, haunted by his fears?

On the contrary, he was warmhearted and humble, obedient to the spiritual and moral disciplines of God. He was courageous and victorious. Something in David's life gave him courage to face and go beyond his fears. His fears served him. He was not dominated by them.

To conquer fear is to have the ability to examine it, learn from it, and move through it to peace and confidence. That's what I mean by finding freedom from fear.

The Benefit of Understanding Fear

Fear has a characteristic that makes it a formidable obstacle. It focuses our attention on immediate feelings and on the object associated with our fear. When we are in its grip we find it difficult to think critically. One of fear's greatest powers is this ability to numb our minds and hearts.

Besides limiting our ability to think clearly, fear colors our perceptions. When we are afraid, everything about life looks more difficult, more menacing, and less secure.

If we are to conquer fear, we must prepare ourselves by clearly understanding what fear is and how it works. This helps us put fear in perspective. Let's consider some concepts related to fear.

Fear and Things Like It

Fear versus cowardice. Cowardice is not a synonym for fear. Cowardice is a reaction to fear.

Do you remember those childhood taunts designed to

make you do something you didn't want to do? If you couldn't jump off the high diving board, for example, you were likely to hear the singsong chant, "David is a scaredy-cat. David is a scaredy-cat." Many of us look back with horror at the feats we performed because of that old chant.

Our culture commonly views cowardice as a character flaw. Even in adulthood this manipulating accusation dominates our lives.

What we must recognize is that being a coward is not the same as feeling afraid. Great heros often admit to having been afraid when they did their heroic acts. Feeling afraid doesn't make you a coward.

What does? Cowardice is withdrawing in the face of fear. It is giving in, instead of going on. Remember this: cowardice is one way of reacting to the presence of fear in your life. Cowardice can prompt us to act in dishonest, treacherous, and shameful ways.

For the time being let's suspend any connotation of shame connected with cowardice. Let's simply say that when we cannot find the wherewithal to get beyond our fear one of the ways we cope is by conceding defeat. The point here is not to berate ourselves if that happens but to find better ways of coping.

Fear versus anger. Like cowardice, anger is sometimes a reaction to fear. Not all anger is caused by fear, but fear can cause anger.

Think what often happens when a child is the butt of a singsong chant. Some children seem to accept it meekly and learn to live with it. Others flare up in anger. "I am not afraid. You're just a bully. I hate you!"

For those who seem to accept the taunt meekly, anger is often harbored deep inside. There it becomes a destructive force, turning into depression and despair.

If cowardice is a faulty way of reacting to fear, so is anger. We become aggressors either against people and circumstances or against ourselves. We cannot adequately confront the sources of our fear when we lash out at others or attack ourselves. Nor can we see constructive ways of dealing with it.

The point is this: anger can be a poor way of coping with fear. It introduces its own destructive influences into the situation and obscures the real issues.

Fear versus worry. Worry is a way of being afraid. Seldom are the specific objects of worry the real causes of fear.

The word *worry* is almost totally attached to mental activity. We think of worry as the state of mind we have when the car payment and electricity bill are both due, the bank balance is low, and our youngest child complains of a toothache.

But worry has another meaning. To worry something is to shake or pull it, work it back and forth, disturb, and tear at it constantly. A dog worries a bone. A cat worries a ball of yarn.

Worry happens when some aspect of life claims our attention. We have some sense of insecurity or threat. We proceed to mull the threat over, disturb it, tear at it, work it back and forth. Worry gets us no closer to a solution; it wastes our mental and emotional resources. It exhausts without solving any problems.

The object of worry is often representative of a deeper issue that makes us feel threatened. To arrive at solutions we must confront those deeper threats.

Fear versus depression. Here's a final distinction before we talk more specifically about fear. Depression is often associated with fear.

Depression can have many causes. One may be a sense of helplessness about some threat we feel unable to handle.

When we're depressed, look out for fear! Every little threat takes on added dimension. Think about what happens when we are ill. Every ache and pain is magnified. Every problem seems more serious.

The same can be true of fears that would not normally bother us. They quickly get out of hand. When we are depressed, we must remember that bad things need to be cut down about three sizes, and that all good things need to be magnified.

How the System Works

Having compared these problems with fear, let's make some practical definitions of fear and discuss the way it works.

Fear is not something that invades us from outside. It isn't a physical substance. It is not a force or a being that takes over our minds.

Instead, fear is a system of internal communication about certain events and circumstances of our lives. It is a mental code, or language, we speak to ourselves based on our interpretations. It is a mental construct.

Let's look at an example of the simplest kind of fear. My parents told me of their narrow escape from a potentially fatal accident. They were driving on an interstate highway. Mother was at the wheel, and Dad was asleep beside her. They droned down the highway, flashing past fields, houses, and signs. Traffic was steady but not heavy.

Suddenly Mother's routine was shattered when a semi-truck pulled out to pass her. The truck driver must have lost sight of her car, because instead of clearing before pulling back into the right lane, he moved directly toward her while the rear wheels of the tractor were just opposite her window.

Mother braked hard and swerved onto the shoulder, barely managing to keep the car from careening out of control. The truck driver went on, completely oblivious to the accident he had almost caused.

26

After bringing the car to a halt she could only sit with her heart in her mouth, shaking uncontrollably, thanking God their lives had been spared. She was so frightened she could not continue driving.

This is an example of the simplest kind of fear. It is easy to see what I mean when I say fear is a mental construct. It's a mental reaction based on past experiences.

An event occurred that Mother interpreted, based on experience, to be terribly threatening. The event was also sudden and severe.

As her mind recorded the event, it did so not just as a spectator but as an interpreter. It asked the meaning of the event, whether it was recognizable, and how it ought to be interpreted. Almost instantly the danger was interpreted, and a response triggered. That interpretation of danger coupled with the mental and physical responses are all part of what we call fear.

The event itself was not the fear. Mother's interpretation and response to a real and clearly perceived threat was the fear.

When we examine more complex kinds of fear, we find this same pattern. There are different kinds of fear, and fears that come from different sources. But whenever we are afraid it is because we have interpreted some event or circumstance as threatening, and our mind prepares for action.

Generally, we use the word *fear* when speaking of our responses to threats that are real, immediate, and clearly perceived. When we speak of responses to imaginary, vague, indirect, or anticipated threats we use the word *anxiety*.

Anxiety is less defined, lasts longer, and is more difficult to conquer than fear. But it's still a kind of fear— something in our life appears threatening. Our minds attempt to warn and prepare us to do something.

How can we think of fear to be prepared for it ahead of

time? I use the image of an alarm system. Anything we interpret to be a threat, whether social, spiritual, psychological, or physical, will set off the alarm.

Seward Hiltner says,

> Anxiety is, so to speak, an alarm clock. It warns of some danger. If it is possible for the person to hear the alarm and then to mobilize his resources, he can do "something to avoid the situation or retreat from it." By fight, flight, or adaptation, he is able, after heeding the alarm, to do something relevant in relation to it. If he succeeds in doing so, then the purpose for which the alarm rang has been fulfilled. The alarm is then stilled until needed again.[1]

How the System Fails

If fear is an alarm system God has given to warn us of danger and prepare us for action, why can it be such a problem? Why must we talk of *conquering* fear?

We must recognize that the world can be threatening. It is a world full of evil, heartache, and illness. There is much to fear in this fallen world.

Fear becomes a problem when the alarm fails to work, or when we aren't prepared to use it correctly. We need to know how the system can fail.

One of the most common malfunctions of the system occurs when we perceive a threat, the alarm is triggered, but for some reason we cannot or will not face the threat. It may be too frightening. We may be unable to think of any way to deal with it. Or we may be unable to identify what threatens us.

In any case the alarm goes on ringing. We feel anxious or afraid, but instead of doing something to take care of the threat, we devise secondary schemes to block out the alarm. Examples of these schemes are alcoholism, compulsive eating, or overwork. Instead of finding and dealing with the threat, we retreat and try to ignore it, project it onto something else, or push it into the future. Eventually this leads to unhealthy and disastrous consequences.

Another way the system malfunctions is when the alarm is triggered by something misinterpreted as threatening (perhaps because of some bad experience in our past). What we think is threatening is not dangerous or, perhaps, doesn't apply to us.

In this case, harmless events may send us into unnecessary agonies of fear. The way out of the problem is to pinpoint what seems to threaten us, confront that event or circumstance head on, and devise constructive ways to deal with it.

How Does This Help?

This understanding of fear can be helpful in a couple ways. It doesn't make fear go away or take away our need for perseverance, courage, and hope in dealing with fear. We may even require professional care. But it does do this for us.

First, it takes away fear's mystery. It no longer seems magical and overpowering. If you know where something is going to hit you and how it is going to hit, you can be prepared.

Second, this view also encourages us to ask questions about our fears instead of just fixating on immediate feelings. When we feel afraid, we know it must be because something presents itself as a threat. We know, then, we must try to discover what that is and take appropriate steps to deal with it.

We can even be thankful for our ability to be afraid, because this ability reminds us of God's care for us. Without a system to alert us of danger we would be terribly vulnerable.

God Meets Us at Our Point of Need

Given this understanding of fear, we can better appreciate the spiritual resources available to us. In particular, we can be thankful for God's assurance that he will meet us at every point of threat. In the midst of fear life can seem dark, but God meets us at our point of need.

Hugh Redwood was busy traveling and meeting public speaking engagements. During a period of particularly heavy responsibility, a very serious problem came into his personal life. His schedule allowed him no rest. He wanted nothing more than to be alone, to think and pray his way through the problem. But each day took him to new places, new homes, and new people. With an aching heart he called on God for help.

At one stop his host seemed unusually sensitive. The host led him to a room where there was a fireplace with a bright fire burning. Beside the fire sat a table and chair. With a few words Mr. Redwood's host excused himself.

Mr. Redwood went to the chair and sat down, gratefully alone. As he sat meditating and praying about his problem, his eyes fell on a Bible that lay open on the table beside him. It was open to the Fifty-ninth Psalm. These words were underlined. "The God of my mercy shall prevent me."

Intrigued, Mr. Redwood read the ancient words of David over and over until their full force began to dawn on him. The warm glow of encouragement poured into his bleak heart. "My God in his lovingkindness *shall meet me at every corner.*"[2]

That is the hope we have in Christ as we deal with fear. He meets us at every corner of our lives. He is there ahead of us. He is there behind us. And his presence makes that particular corner a very different place.

It is his wisdom that gave us the ability to fear. It must be his grace that will give us courage to face fear.

NOTES

[1]Seward Hiltner, "Theories of Anxiety: Psychiatric," *Constructive Aspects of Anxiety*, Eds. Seward Hiltner and Karl Menninger (New York: Abingdon Press, 1963), 26.

[2]Story told in Leslie D. Weatherhead, *Prescription for Anxiety* (New York: Abingdon Press, 1960), 113ff.

3
TAKING THE
INTERACTIVE
APPROACH

Recently a short story in our local newspaper caught my eye. For a long time doctors have used antibiotics to kill bacteria that cause infections and diseases. Drugs that can kill viruses, however, have only recently been discovered.

It seems these new drugs have limited use. Viruses have the ability to develop immunity to these drugs, evolving into super-viruses that no known drug can kill.

This shouldn't surprise anyone. Doctors have known that bacteria have the same ability to evolve into immune strains and thus elude death.

What place does this sort of news have in a book about conquering fear? At the microscopic level of life a principle seems to be at work that is directly related to our experiences of fear. It is the concept of undying hope.

No matter how terrible our experiences of fear,

something in us seeks a way through, a way to survive in spite of the threat.

Living things are threatened with harm, even death. We take these drugs to kill bacteria and viruses that threaten our lives. Sometimes we win and the bacteria and viruses are killed. When they win, we fall ill. Still, in everything alive there is an urge to go on living.

Living things grow old. Strong arms weaken in time. Hearts that beat steadily for years suddenly turn off. Voices once strong quaver with the passing of many words. Eyes that could once pick out a tiny eagle soaring high above a wind-swept ridge mist over, now see only memories.

All of this happens reluctantly. The will to keep going courses through us like a heavenly fire. We know this is true because of the awful change when this inner urge to live disappears.

It's a long way from modern laboratories to the chambers in which David wrote his psalms. But I thought of him when I read the news clipping about antibiotics.

David always found a way through his fears, through the threats, to hope and courage.

This chapter explores the means we have for doing as he did. After all, David's God is ours. The world has changed but people and God have not. If there was courage for David, there is courage for us. If there was hope for him, there is hope for us. Fear may make us feel as though there is none. But there is.

Fear is personal. Each experience of it is a matter of place, time, and circumstance. I cannot offer a cookbook approach for coping with it. I can share some strategies to help conquer it.

Ways to Approach the Problem

When we're wrestling with fear we're in the midst of a battle. Things happen fast. It's often hard to think. The specter of defeat looms over us. It becomes difficult to distinguish reality from fantasy.

By thinking about the problem we gain insight and understanding. We have a better idea of what we're up against and can prepare some weapons to combat future fears.

What are our options for dealing with the problem of fear?

First, we can face fear passively and end up becoming its victims. Cowardice comes into play here. Hope, courage, and confidence disappear. Our fears dominate us. This is not the best approach to handling fear.

Second, we can actively take on fear and become its adversaries. Worry and anger are the results. We lash out, or run in frenzied circles around our problem. But we get no closer to any constructive solution to the threats that cause fear.

We can, and should, face fear interactively. When we do this, we set the stage for conquering it. This is the option I suggest.

The interactive approach uses fear constructively. We challenge it and ask critical questions. We force fear to work for us. What can our fears tell us about ourselves? Where are the danger zones in our lives? Where are the weak areas? In what ways can our fears provide opportunities for growth? How might they be opportunities to see God working in our lives?

We must prepare to take an interactive stance toward fear. We don't want to run from it, lash out at it, or run in frenzied circles around it.

The areas of our lives in which we face fear can become areas of strength. At any rate, that should be our goal.

Here are two keys to the interactive approach.

Interpreting the Alarm

If fear is an alarm triggered when we encounter some real or imagined threat, the first key is to find out exactly what threat has set off the alarm.

When the threat is obvious this may be a straightforward task, as in the case of an impending accident. However, most problem fears aren't clear-cut. When we feel anxious, the threat may be vague, obscured by other factors, or imaginary.

Vague anxiety is a common problem. We aren't afraid as we would be in a hostage situation with someone holding a gun to our heads, but we have a feeling of doom.

Often, instead of challenging this vague anxiety, we struggle with it. We may devise harmless ways of coping— a round of golf, a trip to the mall, or a chat with a friend are enough to distract us.

But specialists tell us fears become unhealthy when we do not pinpoint their causes and learn to take appropriate action. This begins to introduce elements of unreality into our emotional lives and upsets our mental and emotional equilibrium.

Let me give an example. If you've never been to Haiti, I doubt if you can visualize the baggage claim and customs area at the international airport after the arrival of two wide-body jets from the States. But try.

I'll never forget our first arrival. We walked down the stairway off the plane and the heat hit us like a falling wall. A small band played island music just outside the terminal. After a long wait our passports were stamped by a disinterested immigrations official dressed in a neat white shirt and dark blue pants. By then my clothes were wet with sweat. Shifting my carry-on bag from one shoulder to the other, I led my wife and two baby daughters into the baggage claim and customs area.

Taking the Interactive Approach

When we walked through the door of that big room, sanity and courtesy were suddenly suspended. Several hundred sweating, shouting people pushed and elbowed to find a spot in front of the conveyor belts to claim their luggage.

Many possible threats were evident. I immediately responded with a seizure of anxiety. What do I do now?

I posted my wife at one end of the room and laid our carry-on bags at her feet. There were no seats in the room. The floor was dirty. She had the unenviable task of making sure that none of our belongings disappeared in the melee, and that our adventurous three-year-old daughter didn't wander off into some far corner. In her arms she held our six-month-old daughter.

Meanwhile, I jumped into the brawl and caught a couple of well-placed elbows before I found a spot near one conveyor belt. During the next thirty minutes I worked like a madman trying to hold my spot, jerking an occasional piece of luggage off the belt, and watching to make sure the pieces I stacked behind me didn't melt into the crowd.

By the time I collected all our belongings, the girls were crying, Helen was close to it, and I was beside myself. But all our pieces still had to be passed through customs. That meant they had to be hoisted, one by one, onto a counter and opened for the inspector to rummage through.

All of this took place with hundreds of people in the same frenzy to get through the process—pushing, elbowing, shouting.

After I got all the bags lifted to the counter, opened, closed again, and piled onto the floor on the other side, a skycap put them on his cart.

However, I was far from done. Next I had to find an official to verify that these bags were a part of our incoming freight, so we wouldn't have to pay a special duty. I needn't have bothered. No one there knew what I was talking about. It took me an hour to find that out.

By the time we finished, all four of us were completely exhausted. But it was time to meet our new colleagues and friends. We wondered what impression we could possibly be making.

I learned to hate customs and baggage claim. Many of the supplies and tools used for our ministry were imported, since they were unavailable or too expensive to purchase locally. Of course, my trips in and out of the country also took me through baggage claim and customs. We never knew what the inspectors would seize. It took forever to get whatever they did seize out of customs, and then a high price in duty fees usually had to be paid.

If thoughts of customs and baggage claim didn't squeeze my stomach into a knot beforehand, I was always a wreck after the process.

How did I cope? I usually got irritable and strident. I would resolve to stay cool, not to let the experience get to me. But that never worked.

Afterward I would berate myself. Why didn't I have the self-control not to get rattled, not to say angry words to inspectors when they were insolent or threatened to take things from my bags?

Not until I began to trace the source of my feelings did I begin to cope better with customs and baggage claim. When I thought about it, it was easy to see that my fear of losing our belongings in the heat and frenzy of the situation was at the root of my actions. This seems blazingly obvious in retrospect, but it was not immediately clear to me. The experience was hectic, frantic, physically uncomfortable, and time-consuming. Only when I began to think critically, to take an interactive approach to the situation, did I realize that almost every one of my responses grew out of threats I felt. Fear was at the root of my inability to cope.

It did no good to berate myself for my reactions. Only when I identified the threats was I able to change responses.

Here then is a central key. Dealing with fear interactively requires searching out and clarifying the threats that trigger our fear. This process requires insight and practice. Sometimes we may need help to accomplish this.

Prayer can be a wonderful source of help. I have found that prayerful meditation and reflection gives God the opportunity to illuminate areas in my life that have seemed obscure. He also uses Scripture to provide such insight. Issues that have been unclear come into focus, and I see my life with new perspective.

Another source of help is the counsel of a trusted friend. Friends who know us well, demonstrate godly wisdom, and in whom we have confidence, can be an important benefit. Since they are not wrestling with our fear, they bring a clearer perspective to the problem. Sometimes just talking through our experiences of fear with someone brings us new insights.

Professional counselors can be valuable aids if our anxieties get beyond our ability to cope. We need not assume that every anxiety is related to some subconscious cause, but it is not unusual for surface fears to be manifestations of deeper threats. In these cases, professional care is helpful and often necessary.

Professional counselors will do what I have suggested here. They will try to help us work through our symptoms to find their sources and will then help us devise ways of coping.

Some researchers say as many as eleven million Americans a year suffer from anxiety disorders. If our fears are beyond our ability to cope, we should not feel alone or hesitate to get professional help.

However, many of our fears are within our capacity to

cope. We can find both relief and courage by pinpointing the threat that triggers our fear alarm.

Devising a Plan

Pinpointing the threat is helpful, but the reason for doing so is to help us lay out a plan for dealing with the threat. This is the second key in approaching fear interactively.

We often deal with fear by trying to make our bad feelings go away. We attack the emotion, while leaving its cause untouched.

But if fear is an alarm to warn us of danger, the last thing we want to do is shut off the alarm without eliminating the danger. That's simply an invitation to disaster.

I first learned to take this interactive approach when I left high school and went to college.

I was born and grew up in the Philippine islands. I was fourteen and ready for tenth grade when my family moved back to the midwestern United States. I was far more Filipino than American at that point, even though I had spent five years attending an American school in Manila.

Because of our extensive travel, my world included regular trips across the Pacific. I had visited Hong Kong, Japan, and Hawaii several times. I knew all about carabaos and rice paddies. I traveled regularly by jeepney and bus around Manila, a city of several million people. Swimming in Lingayen Bay and the South China Sea had been part of my experience. My cousins and I had explored the exciting slopes high in the mountains of northern Luzon.

Suddenly I was thrown into a world that, though wonderful and intriguing, was totally foreign. It often seemed the circle of reference of my peers extended no farther than fifty miles from our town. The highlights of their lives were cars, members of the opposite sex, and basketball.

I became frozen with fear as I faced this new country, a new school, and new friends. In my new school, my class alone numbered over eight hundred. My previous school had had no more than three hundred students in kindergarten through grade twelve. I felt out of place, so odd and so lonely. This was not my world.

To make matters worse, I was in the bloom of awkward adolescence—clumsy, with wiry, unruly hair, and pimpled face. My social skills were attuned to Philippine society, not midwestern America.

My peers' conversation ran to girls, cars, sports, and parties (both tame and otherwise). I could only talk about countries they had never seen and could not understand.

The task of making friends petrified me, so I kept to myself. I learned to make myself invisible to avoid having to talk to anyone. Only after two years did I begin to make a few friends. High school was a miserable, frightening experience.

When I finally escaped and thought of attending college, I made myself one promise. If I never graduated, I would at least make friends!

This would not be easy. I would have to overcome my shyness and fear of being around new people. As I thought about high school, I asked why I had been so afraid to make friends. I began to see a connection between this fear, my poor self-image, and the process of dislocation I had endured after ninth grade. These experiences had given me a terrible inner habit.

My internal commentary always ran like this: "No one wants to talk to you. You're just a strange, ugly missionary kid. Who wants to be your friend? You're not hip. You don't have a fancy car. You're not witty, polished, good looking, or smart. Mind your own business. No one wants to look at you or talk to you."

No wonder I was afraid of people! I kept myself continually convinced everyone despised me. The first key was to discover the source of my social fears—I had internalized a terrible self-image because of a process of dislocation that came at a vulnerable time in my life. I feared being humiliated, being unable to function in this new place. I feared rejection.

Arriving at this understanding without moving further would have left me mired in self-pity. The next step was to devise a plan to follow at college.

One part of my plan was to do whatever I could to make myself more attractive. But more importantly, I decided to develop a new internal commentary. Even if it were true that others found me ugly, uninteresting, and socially inept, the only chance I had of breaking through those barriers was to get to know people, and let them get to know me. In order to have the courage to do that I made myself repeat an inner dialogue that went like this:

"You are an interesting person. Think of all the places you've been! Think of all the things you have to talk about—exploring street shops in Hong Kong, climbing mountains in the Philippines, eating roasted dog meat! So you're not the greatest looking person in the world, but you're not that bad. People will be glad to get to know you. They need friends too. They're probably just as hungry for friendship as you are."

Over several months, my plan began to help. As I worked my way through this process, I began to conquer some of the anxieties that had always kept me from reaching out to others.

That doesn't mean all my social fears vanished. But I was able to move through them to courage and friendship. The painful memories of the past could no longer dictate my behavior. I made many friends and enjoyed their company.

I share this story to illustrate that when we can pinpoint the reasons for our fear, we can devise plans of action to help us deal with those sources, not just with the emotions we feel.

Unfortunately we often don't take advantage of this process.

A friend of mine took a new job in a highly competitive sales environment. The field was new to him, so he had lots of learning to do. At the same time, he felt he wasn't going to be given long to prove his ability to sell.

After several days I stopped by and we chatted over lunch. He was feeling anxious. Was he doing well enough? Was his boss about to fire him? Should he have taken another job?

Instead of wringing his hands and worrying, a much more productive approach was to clarify the sources of his anxiety and devise a plan to keep him going.

We both knew that. But when we're in the middle of fear, we tend to lose our ability to clearly reason. We fail to do what will help us most.

The problem was not that my friend couldn't determine the source of his anxiety. Rather, he needed help to face fear interactively.

I encouraged him in this way. His ability to sell had not deserted him. He had proven that before. This was a new field. He needed to learn the product, keep making presentations, and refuse to play mind games about his boss's pleasure or displeasure. No level-headed future employer would fault him if he got fired for failing to produce at top speed without having had the chance to learn a new field.

The second key to the interactive approach is to move beyond an understanding of the sources of our fears to devising ways to directly deal with those threats. Unless we make this a habit, we may get stuck reacting to negative emotions, instead of solving the underlying problems that produce fear.

Two final points. First, some of our fears are clear-cut—they come from threats that are real and unambiguous. Others are vague—their sources more difficult to determine. Finding sources of fear and making a plan of action will not necessarily erase all our emotions, but we will be on our way to moving through them to courage and confidence.

Second, sometimes fears are tied to psychological or physical causes. Nervous exhaustion and physical illness may introduce fear into our lives. Chemical imbalances can produce many kinds of anxiety disorders. We should consider these physiological and psychological sources. Doctors report that 75 to 90 percent of those who suffer from anxiety disorders respond well to treatment. Unfortunately, less than 25 percent seek professional help.[1]

We shouldn't hesitate to get competent professional care if our fears are debilitating or are more than we can handle.

Let's Review

Let's review what we've discussed and describe where we're going.

Fear is an alarm system given by our Creator to warn us of impending danger. As such, it is harmless. In fact, it is a great blessing.

Problems arise when the alarm fails, or when we misuse it. We get into trouble if we don't, or can't, do anything about the threat that triggered the alarm. Fear becomes a problem if the alarm rings unnecessarily, or if we can't get the alarm to stop even when we've dealt with the threat.

The best approach to anxiety is to clarify the source of those feelings. Do we need to deal with some clear-cut threat? Are there recurring mental images and thoughts that make us feel anxious? If so, our mental alarm is trying to alert us to problems that need to be addressed.

After clarifying the source of anxiety, we devise a plan of action. If the threat is clear-cut and physical, we eliminate it or prepare to defend ourselves. If the source is disturbing mental images and thoughts, we can question and modify these. Where did they come from? Are they associated with memories? Are they realistic? Should they be the sole authority? Are there other ways of looking at life and the situation?

Armed with this understanding of fear and this simple process, we are ready to take a new direction in our study. Taking these steps requires courage, perspective, and hope. The great blessing of our spiritual life is this: in all these tasks, our walk with God contributes stability, courage, and hope.

Remember our God-given urge to live (my little story about the viruses and bacteria)? Our ability to fear is actually part of that urge to live. God gave it to us so we could live well.

Unfortunately, we live in a fallen world and suffer the effects of that fall. Fear often becomes a problem. Our stores of hope and courage run dangerously low. That's when we need to use the resources our daily walk with God provides to help us conquer fear.

NOTES

[1]"Anxiety Attacks: Success in Halting the Frightening Cycle," *Regarding Women and Healthcare* (Lexington: The University of Kentucky Hospital, Winter, 1989), 1.

4

RAISING COURAGE
IN THE SANCTUARY
OF GOD'S PRESENCE

THE NEED: To conquer fear we need courage.

THE RESOURCE: The sanctuary of God's presence is a resource for courage because it is a refuge in which we prepare to face the sources of our fears.

We need five things in order to conquer fear—courage, stability, perspective, comfort, and hope. All of these must be present to some degree to cope well with the fear-inducing threats that are a normal part of life. Most therapists try to help provide all five for their patients.

Where do we find these elements? In the next five chapters we'll discuss the resources made available by our walk with God. These resources provide exactly what we need for a life of peace and confidence.

Remember, fear isn't something we can "get over" with the right treatment or the right medicine. We can get over specific problems that cause us anxiety, but we set ourselves up for despair if we hold the notion we will never feel anxious or afraid.

We can't expect life to be without anxiety, but we can plan on peace and confidence. The resources provided by our walk with God provide us an inner stability and strength. These will allow us to take life in stride.

In this chapter we'll discuss the first element—courage. Courage has to do with the way we respond to those real or imagined threats. Courage is not deadness to the danger.

Courage: Testing Our Mettle

The importance of courage was impressed on me one very unpleasant day in Haiti.

Haiti's one paved highway system runs from the old colonial city of Cap Haitien on the north coast, south to Port-au-Prince, and from there west and south to Jacmel and Les Cayes—two fine old towns on the south coast. Virtually all travel throughout the country depends on this highway.

Foreigners might think a small, poor country like Haiti would not need the road very much. But the opposite is true. Travel is vital because so much of the food, clothing, and other supplies people depend on are manufactured or imported at Port-au-Prince. This means people must either travel there to buy their needs or rely on local merchants to transport the supplies from Port-au-Prince to rural areas.

During the overthrow of the Duvalier regime, the common people's chief means of civil disobedience was to close this highway. Groups would gather at strategic locations and build barricades of burning tires and other debris.

These roadblocks were volatile, highly charged scenes. Those who built and manned the roadblocks would often be drunk with *tafia* and overcome with the heady experience of wielding such unaccustomed power.

One week, I promised Pastor Dumont I would visit his church in the town of St. Michelle de l'Attalaye. St. Michelle is a small, dusty provincial town in the middle of a wide, arid plateau that is crossed by a lazy river and dotted with scrub bushes. To reach it means traveling over a dirt road that branches from the main highway out into the plain. The trip from my home to St. Michelle, about 120 miles, would take six to eight hours.

Pastor Dumont was eager for us to visit the church. There were new converts to be baptized, and the congregation was looking forward to building a new sanctuary.

The day we had set for the trip turned out to be one of the most riotous weekends of the year. Protestors went on rampages all over the country attacking government officials and their families, burning buildings and vehicles, and closing roads.

There was a further complication. Pastor Dumont had served as the education secretary for St. Michelle, a link to the Duvalier government that almost proved fatal. During an earlier rampage, protestors had tried to capture and kill him, even though no one could think of any wrong he had done. Pastor Dumont had narrowly escaped and fled into hiding. He planned to use the occasion of our trip to return home, hoping that by arriving in the company of several ministers, at least one of whom was an American, no one would dare attack him. I found this notion unsettling to say the least.

Pastor Dumont showed up at my home early on the day of our trip. Despite the violence and unrest, he was eager to be off. I was very hesitant to go. Roadblocks had been set up all around the country. Our own town was incredibly tense. Several people had been killed in demonstrations a few days earlier. I was afraid to make the trip considering the reception we might receive at St. Michelle, the danger of traveling through numerous roadblocks, and the danger of leaving my family at home alone.

However, Pastor Dumont was adamant. He reminded me of the new converts waiting to be baptized and of his own need to return home. We simply must go, he said.

Finally, in spite of my uneasiness, and against what I thought was better judgment, I agreed. We loaded our truck. Pastor Dumont, a student from his congregation, and a dozen or so other students, friends, and neighbors who wanted a lift to various spots, climbed aboard. I could not conceal my uneasiness and my reluctance to go.

As we were leaving, a young woman student of mine turned to me and said, "Pasteur, nou ta dwe oue ou sans crainte." "Pastor, we should see you without fear."

For a moment, her words took my breath away. I didn't know what to say. I felt guilty, embarrassed, and angry all at once. Mumbling something about the difference between bravery and good judgment I drove on, full of conflicting emotions.

My student's words had not only pinpointed my fear, but had touched a raw nerve. Instead of clearly thinking through the options and making a wise choice, my mind and heart were jumbled. I felt mixed up, paralyzed, and ashamed. Where was my courage?

As it turned out, we didn't get far. We met our first roadblock thirty-five miles down the road. It was a scene of violent pandemonium. Angry threats were exchanged between drivers and those manning the roadblock. Bottles and rocks flew back and forth across the road. Burning tires and other debris blocked the way.

As I inched forward, a tall young man with a long pole came up to my window and said, "Don't worry, Pastor. When I move the barrier, drive through quickly." I nodded my head. After he moved a couple of tires with his pole, I drove over the remaining debris as quickly as possible and went on.

A mile or so ahead I could see huge billows of black smoke rolling hundreds of feet into the air. As we drove slowly toward it, four young men appeared at the side of the road brandishing huge rocks, motioning for us to stop. When I did they climbed onto the truck and yelled, "Don't worry, pastor, we'll get you through for fifty dollars."

With that my resolve disappeared. Turning the truck around, I bluntly told Pastor Dumont that it was foolish to continue under those conditions. He got out of the truck in disgust and went off to find another ride. I turned the truck around and headed home.

Back at the first roadblock the mob had stopped a large delivery truck and was busy helping themselves to its cargo. We squeezed through a spot in the barricade and continued on.

All the while my student's words kept going through my head. "Pastor, we should see you without fear."

What did it mean to have courage in that situation? Where could I go to find it? Experiences like these demand answers because they probe you, making you wonder what you're made of.

Courage is defined as "mental or moral strength to venture, persevere, and withstand danger, fear, or difficulty."[1] It "implies firmness of mind and will in the face of danger or extreme difficulty."[2]

Courage would not necessarily have made me follow through with my trip to St. Michelle in spite of the dangers. Perhaps in those circumstances, bravado would have made me do that. But courage would have pushed aside my jumbled thinking, paralysis, and shame. It would have given me the ability to think more clearly about the whole situation, to pinpoint the issues at stake, and to come to a wise course of action.

Mettle is a synonym sometimes used in place of courage. We talk of having our mettle tested. "Mettle suggests an ingrained capacity for meeting strain or difficulty with fortitude and resilience."[3]

That's the essence of courage—an ingrained capacity for meeting strain or difficulty with fortitude and resilience. Notice the important points.

This capacity is ingrained. We aren't necessarily born with it. It's something we train into ourselves. We develop the capacity to run long distances by training and habit. We develop fortitude and resilience in the same way.

Courage isn't something that's dumped in our laps. It can't be produced by artificial substances. It's up to us to produce it, to choose it.

When we have anxiety or fear, we feel as though that particular threat is going to demolish us. Catastrophe looms over us. But when we have courage we can bounce back. It gives us staying power.

Courage puts anxiety on hold and says, "I hear the alarm. Now let's see what's really going on and what needs to be done."

Raising Courage

The question remains: how do we raise courage when our minds are a jumble of panic-stricken thoughts, and our hearts sink deeper and deeper into fear?

Here is where one of our spiritual resources proves most beneficial. My experience on the road to St. Michelle was one of several that taught me volumes about the sanctuary of God's presence. Whatever courage I could muster in those desperate days came from this special place of refuge.

At the rear of my house was a small utility room that I turned into my prayer room. I would go there during those lowest times and pour out my jumbled thoughts in prayer. Sometimes I would cover my head with a towel to muffle the sound of my voice so as not to disturb others. I went there to muster courage. The location was not as important as the spiritual reality it represented.

It is hard to put into words the courage that comes from sensing you are in God's very presence. I felt wrapped in a warm glow. The knot in my chest would give way to a feeling of relaxation. The urgent clamor of my fears would be replaced by peace in the sanctuary of God's presence.

Here is the wonderful secret of this spiritual resource. When gripped by anxiety, we can see no alternatives to the catastrophe that looms in our minds. We can't raise courage by challenging that catastrophe. That's why it does no good to tell ourselves, or to be told by others, to take courage. We can't. We need something else.

Remember, courage is an ingrained habit. Courage comes as we develop the habit of choosing to focus our thoughts on something that has the power to replace our fears. In this way we release our minds from the monopoly of anxiety.

We do not raise courage by thumbing our noses at the threats of life but by choosing to turn to the sanctuary of God's presence. This shifts our attention from the focus of our anxiety to a source of courage.

How does this work? Let's look at an example of David's responses to fearful circumstances.

The Importance of Choice

David's psalms show an interesting routine, a habitual way of responding to the threats in his life. Here's an example.

In the LORD I take refuge.
How then can you say to me:
"Flee like a bird to your mountain.
For look, the wicked bend their bows;
they set their arrows against the strings
to shoot from the shadows
at the upright in heart.
When the foundations are being destroyed,
what can the righteous do?"

The LORD is in his holy temple;
the LORD is on his heavenly throne.
He observes the sons of men;
his eyes examine them.
The LORD examines the righteous,
but the wicked and those who love violence
his soul hates.
On the wicked he will rain
fiery coals and burning sulfur;
a scorching wind will be their lot.

For the LORD is righteous,
he loves justice;
upright men will see his face.

(Psalm 11)

This psalm illustrates the approach we have been discussing. First, David identified the threat that troubled him. In this case, he was evidently facing intense personal, and perhaps national, attack. Not only was he under attack, but some people around him seemed to make the problem worse by telling him to run and hide.

Second, notice the way David weighs the options open to him. Where would he draw his strength?

In this psalm David mimicked those who told him to hide. Some said, "Run away quickly to your mountain fortress. Bar yourself in. That's the only place you'll be safe.

After all, when the foundations of life are breaking up, what can you expect? Look, your enemies have their arrows on their bowstrings! Better run."

Anxiety always sounds that way. It's urgent. There seems no good solution.

But to these suggestions David firmly replied, "I take refuge in the Lord. The Lord is in his holy temple, and on his throne. I turn to him. How can you counsel me to seek out some other security?"

This does not mean David did nothing else to deal with threatening circumstances. We know from other biblical records that he fought his enemies with great success. When he could not win Saul over, he was forced to run from him for a while. When David's own son Absalom attempted to dethrone him, though depression and anguish made David passive for a long time, he eventually took practical steps to deal with the threat.

But in David's distress and fear, his first response was to turn to the sanctuary of God's presence. He repeatedly chose the way illustrated in these verses.

O LORD my God, *I take refuge in you;*
    save and deliver me from all who pursue me,
or they will tear me like a lion
    and rip me to pieces with no one to rescue me.
(7:1–2)

The LORD is a refuge for the oppressed,
    a stronghold in times of trouble.
Those who know your name will trust in you,
    for you, LORD, have never forsaken those who
      seek you.
(9:9–10)

Some trust in chariots and some in horses,
    but *we trust in the name of the LORD our God.*
(20:7)

David illustrates the spiritual resource we have for courage. One of the lessons we must learn about anxiety is the importance of choice. When anxiety strikes we forget we can make some choices. We may be unable to make the bad feelings go away immediately, and we may be unable to make the threat disappear, but we can make the simple choice of what to do next.

When anxiety comes, make it a habit to suspend those initial panic-stricken thoughts, and first turn to the sanctuary of God's presence. In that sanctuary, bring those fears to God.

Making this choice moves us one step away from our fears. It gives us a chance to view them from a little distance and, in this way, removes some of their power.

There's another important fact here. When we talk of choosing to respond to anxiety by entering the sanctuary of God's presence, we aren't talking about a psychological gimmick.

Sanctuary: A Place Set Apart

The nature of this particular sanctuary sets this spiritual resource apart from any other.

What is a sanctuary? In English that word is related to words like *sanctify*, *sacrosanct*, and *saint*. If we trace these words to their Latin sources, and then to Greek, we find they have a common root. That root is the same as the root of the word *holy*.

To sanctify something is to make it holy. A saint is one who is holy. A sanctuary is a holy place.

What then does it mean to be holy? In its simplest sense, to be holy is to be set apart or uncommon. A set apart thing, place, or person, is set apart for some purpose.

For example, a wildlife sanctuary is set aside for animals. Nothing is allowed into it that is injurious to animals, or contrary to the nature and interests of animals.

Calling God's presence a sanctuary means it is a place set apart in which only those persons and things that conform to God's nature can exist.

In David's psalms about distress and fear he is focused on the sanctuary of God's presence as a holy place. He goes on to describe the nature of this holiness. This is a sanctuary in which life is sacred—it protects and enlivens. It is a sanctuary in which love is supreme—it heals. It is a sanctuary in which "rightness" reigns—it instructs.

LORD, who may dwell in your sanctuary?
  Who may live on your holy hill?

He whose walk is blameless
  and who does what is righteous,
who speaks the truth from his heart
  and has no slander on his tongue,
who does his neighbor no wrong
  and casts no slur on his fellow man,
who despises a vile man
  but honors those who fear the LORD,
who keeps his oath
  even when it hurts,
who lends his money without usury
  and does not accept a bribe against the
    innocent.

He who does these things
  will never be shaken.

                              (Psalm 15)

What type of person is welcome in the sanctuary of God's presence?

Those who belong in this sanctuary live out the twin virtues of "faith in" and "obedience to" God. God asks that we engage in a living give-and-take.

Those who belong in this sanctuary live according to

his moral will. They speak the truth willingly. They refrain from slander. They do no wrong to their neighbors. They carefully choose to honor those who fear God. They keep their word even when it hurts. They refuse to do anything that would bring others into financial bondage. They do not subvert justice by accepting bribes.

Notice the themes here. If we want access to the sanctuary of God's presence we have two basic responsibilities. The first is to live in right relationship with God—in faith and obedience. The second is to live in charity and harmony with our fellow human beings.

This is what makes the sanctuary of God's presence a powerful source of courage. To enter it means that we have an inner sense of rightness. To enter it also means that we enjoy the nature and the protection of the God who defines it.

The sanctuary of God's presence is a special place, a place set apart for those who know God, love him, and walk in step with his will. What makes it a strong resource of courage is not just our choosing but the object of our choice.

When we choose the sanctuary of God's presence, we can say with David,

> Keep me safe, O God,
>   for in you I take refuge.
>
> I said to the LORD, "You are my Lord;
>   apart from you I have no good thing."
>
> The sorrows of those will increase
>   who run after other gods.
> I will not pour out their libations of blood
>   or take up their names on my lips.
>
> LORD, you have assigned me my portion and my
>   cup;
>   you have made my lot secure.

The boundary lines have fallen for me in pleasant
    places;
    surely I have a delightful inheritance.

I will praise the LORD, who counsels me;
    even at night my heart instructs me.
I have set the LORD always before me.
    Because he is at my right hand,
I will not be shaken.

Therefore my heart is glad and my tongue
    rejoices;
    my body also will rest secure,
because you will not abandon me to the grave,
    nor will you let your Holy One see decay.

You have made known to me the path of life;
    you will fill me with joy in your presence,
    with eternal pleasures at your right hand.
                 (Psalm 16)

Where do we turn when fear comes? We all have
places of safety, refuges we instinctively run to when
anxiety comes.

For some that refuge is material—so much money in
the bank, a secure job, a home. Some climb into the
security of a bottle of alcohol. Some turn to doctors, and
others to various kinds of physical distractions.

In the sanctuary of God's presence we can be ourselves. Our anxieties do not disqualify us from love, do not
lower our worth, or represent problems too big to handle.

We don't enter this sanctuary to run away from fears
or to make fears disappear. That's a common misconcep-
tion of the help God gives in facing daily life. We want to
believe that God will somehow lift us right out of the
rugged circumstances of life. We want him to make the bad
experiences go away.

Sometimes he does. Sometimes he intervenes and brings special healing or miraculous deliverance from difficult circumstances. He always watches over us, monitoring the course of our lives, guarding and guiding. For this we are supremely grateful.

But many times he doesn't lift us out of difficulty. Instead, when we turn to the sanctuary of God's presence he seems to give new reserves of courage to face daily life. With these attributes, we pass through the events of life in peace.

Orlando M. F. Caetano knew what it was like to be without sanctuary. Listen to his description of childhood. "Fear flooded my young mind," he said. "I tried hard to hide it, but nothing I did removed the icy feeling that gripped me. My parents were religious, but their religion was rooted in superstition and mysticism. At times they would tell me about strange spirits and satanic visions. The trauma of these tales terrorized my days and nights."

"My church offered no help. Although I was bodily present in the church building, I may as well have been absent. Nothing I saw or heard spoke to my heart, calmed my fears, or wiped away my doubts and insecurity."

But then a miracle happened in Orlando's life. He was given a Bible, and as he read it, he found the way into the sanctuary of God's presence. In his simple words is clothed the massive truth of salvation and courage that sanctuary brings.

"As I read," he said, "the living Word crept into my heart." He was set free from his fear, and a new courage was born within him.[4]

Perhaps Stinnette has said it best. "The resolution of anxiety is a fruit of Christian faith. It comes as a gift, while we are preoccupied with entering into the joy of our heavenly Father."[5]

NOTES

[1]*Webster's Seventh New Collegiate Dictionary* (Springfield, MA: G. & C. Merriam Company, Publishers, 1971).

[2]Ibid.

[3]Ibid.

[4]Orlando M. F. Caetano, "Freedom From Fear," *Evangelizing Today's Child*, Vol. 12 (July 1985), 71.

[5]Charles R. Stinnette, Jr., *Anxiety and Faith: Toward Resolving Anxiety in Christian Community* (Greenwich, Connecticut: The Seabury Press, 1955), 4.

5
BUILDING A STABLE
LIFE FOUNDATION

THE NEED: To conquer fear we need a stable life foundation.

THE RESOURCE: God's grace allows forgiveness, healing, and self-acceptance. With these he helps us build a stable foundation.

One leading therapist has this to say about the root of anxiety. "Anxiety is always characterized by a sense of vulnerability. The danger may be psychological: the threat of humiliation, disapproval, rejection, abandonment, exposure of one's weaknesses. Or it may be physical."[1] To these ideas we could add the danger posed by moral failure.

At the center of the emotional and physical sensations connected with our fears we find the feeling of vulnerability to some unwanted or dangerous event.

There's much that makes us feel vulnerable. For example, a dear friend of mine has a career in which liability suits are common. She is conscientious, careful, and very good at what she does, but carries with her a constant sense of vulnerability to the trauma and cost of being sued. This vulnerability brings much fear into her working life.

Parents know the vulnerability that comes with setting teenage children free to make choices about their lives.

Executives know the vulnerability of competition in the marketplace. Can they produce? Will they be replaced by the "young bucks" eager for their jobs? Will they be pushed aside in their prime?

Vulnerability was one of the issues that led me to reexamine my faith in God. Could that faith really help me deal with my insecurities?

Facing Vulnerability

Mike and Ron and their families were missionary friends who lived near us in Haiti.[2] As was often the case in those days of political turmoil, Mike, Ron, and I were talking about the disturbing events we had witnessed or experienced. The chaos of the judicial system was our topic of the day.

Ron had recently come through a terribly frightening event. One of his trips had taken him to the capital city of Port-au-Prince. That afternoon, after running several errands, he started down Delmas Avenue in his small pickup truck.

You must understand that driving in Haiti is not like driving in the United States. The road is shared by pedestrians, heavily laden two-wheeled carts pulled by one or two men, donkeys, bicycles, motorcycles, and all sorts of vehicles. There is little or no traffic control: People do whatever seems to fit their purposes at the moment.

Delmas Avenue is a long street that runs from the town of Petionville high on the mountains above Port-au-Prince, curving down to the bay. On this particular day rain began to fall. The road became slick, and pedestrians scattered here and there seeking shelter.

Suddenly a woman darted out from the left curb, head down, shielding her eyes from the rain with her hand. Before Ron could react, the woman ran into his truck door, bounced up and hit her head on the cap that covered the back of the truck, then fell limply on the street.

Ron stopped his truck and ran to see how badly she was injured. He watched with horror as she died almost instantly.

To stay at the scene of such an accident in Haiti is to invite serious injury and even death. Relatives of the victim often retaliate by attacking the driver of the vehicle. A Haitian friend urged Ron to go the nearest police station and report the accident. Ron, his wife, teenage son, and their Haitian friend all made their way to the station.

What followed turned into an extended nightmare. They were all imprisoned for several hours while the authorities decided what to do. As they waited, a prison guard went from person to person pounding his rifle butt on their toes. Next he took Ron's pen and began writing on his wife's leg, pushing her dress higher and higher until she finally brushed his hand away in disgust. He laughed derisively and went away.

They were eventually released, but Ron's truck was seized and he was charged with first-degree homicide. Through a long series of legal processes Ron's lawyers were able to get the charges reduced so that he was required to pay several fines. But for many months, the family faced vulnerability wondering what would happen to them.

During the long ordeal I prayed for Ron and his family and did what I could to help. They were not alone. The tragedy is that such accidents happened all the time.

Another friend had a similar accident days before he and his family were scheduled to leave the country for an extended vacation. When he went to report the accident he was stripped and put into a cell. The bare concrete block cell he was held in had no facilities. The stench was so powerful he had to breathe by burying his face under his arm. The accident was not his fault, but he was imprisoned until he agreed to pay several thousand dollars in "fines" to a local judge.

As Ron, Mike, and I rehashed these stories, I could feel fear rising within me. My work required much travel throughout the country. For months when I left my home in the morning, I felt certain I would not come home that evening—that I would die in an accident, or be taken to prison. I would not let my wife drive unless it was absolutely necessary, for fear of what would happen if she had an accident.

I don't wish to multiply lurid stories, but I could tell many more. My point is to illustrate the sense of fear that gripped me as I realized how vulnerable we all were to tragedy. Years later, when I recall those events, my stomach still tightens and my hands shake.

Coping requires finding a way to face the sense of vulnerability that lies behind our anxiety. The easiest way to do this is to eliminate the circumstance that triggers vulnerability. But this isn't always possible—there will always be events that make us feel vulnerable.

Instead of an escape, we need a solid foundation from which to face and resolve vulnerabilities that arise. Just as in our need for courage, the Christian life makes a unique and powerful contribution at exactly this point. We need patience to work through problems that may not quickly disappear. We need a certainty that we will get through, no matter how bad things look at the moment.

We have a good chance of working through vulnerabilities and fears with this inner stability. Without it, we are in danger.

Secure Foundations

The message of the Bible is not that faith in God brings exemption from vulnerability. This world remains a frightening place. We have to live in it even when we walk with God. Unfortunately, we can get caught in the trap of trying to figure out why God, in his love and mercy, allows us to face the frightening events of life.

If we stop here, we miss the message of the Bible, and the greatest blessing of life in Christ. The good news is more complex, closer to the real world, and more comforting than the utopian hope of exemption from vulnerability.

Living in Christ is not an escape hatch. It is an ongoing relationship with a living, caring Being who keeps us always in his thoughts and forever in his love. It is a personal life, an individual pilgrimage.

I like the old English word *conversation* that the King James Version uses for this life with God. Today we talk in terms of relationships, or of our daily walk.

The Christian life is a shared experience, an ongoing conversation carried out in word, thought, and deed between two mutually committed individuals. I love the imagery in that word.

As a child of God I am not adrift, isolated in a world of vast and inscrutable forces. Instead, God and I walk together through the many twists and turns of life. In shady pastures and beside still waters, he is with me; in deep, dark valleys, and in the shadows of death and desperation, the conversation still goes on.

In this conversation, this life shared with God, I have

two priceless treasures. I have the chance to deal with the very deepest nature and source of my human vulnerability. I have a solid foundation to rely on as I face the deep, dark valleys through which my way sometimes leads.

Two crucial exchanges take place in this life. From them comes the security of a stable life foundation.

Grace for Guilt

Fear first appears in the Bible in the Garden of Eden, after Adam and Eve disobey God.

I find it significant that the first time we're introduced to the concept of fear in Scripture, we don't see it applied to human relationships. Adam and Eve did not fear each other. Neither do we see it applied to the relationship between the humans and the natural world. Adam and Eve were not afraid of the animals or of the powerful forces of nature.

The first fear came into the world in the relationship between humankind and God. After their sin, Adam and Eve hid themselves. When God found them, Adam said, "I was afraid."

Here are some interesting points in the Bible's treatment of fear. First, fear is often used to describe the emotions with which people approach God and enter his presence. This fear of God is of two types. One is a guilty fear—the kind Adam felt. The other is a reverential fear—something like awe or worship.

Second, guilty fear was originally tied to moral failure, as in the case of Adam and Eve. People felt this way before God when they knew they had fallen short of his desires. This inner sense of vulnerability before God is undoubtedly one of the reasons for the depression and anxiety of our world.

Many of us cannot pinpoint the reason for that aching, unsettled feeling inside. We blame it on boredom, pressure, or a thousand other things. In reality, it is another way in which our God-given alarm attempts to warn us of danger—in this case, spiritual danger.

I say guilty fear was *originally* tied to moral failure, because just as our minds can be mistaken about other dangers, they can be mistaken about this danger. Our alarm may be triggered by an imagined rather than a real threat. Even after we have accepted God's solution for our moral failures, that is, repentance and faith in Christ, it is possible for our minds to go on ringing the alarm of guilty fear. In such a case we need to treat this fear just as we would any other. We need to pinpoint the problem (not moral failure but faulty ways of thinking about ourselves and about God) and plan a realistic course of action to take care of it.

Third, guilty fear encompasses a related problem. Moral failure damages other spheres of human life so new vulnerabilities spring up. Not only do we feel an inner sense of guilt and vulnerability toward God, but our moral failures often stir up anger, resentment, and hurt among our neighbors.

David often wrote his psalms around these ideas. The Thirty-eighth Psalm is a good example. Let's look at some of its verses.

> O LORD, do not rebuke me in your anger
>   or discipline me in your wrath.
> For your arrows have pierced me,
>   and your hand has come down upon me.
> Because of your wrath there is no health in my
>   body;
>   my bones have no soundness because of my sin.
> My guilt has overwhelmed me
>   like a burden too heavy to bear.
>
> My wounds fester and are loathsome
>   because of my sinful folly.
> I am bowed down and brought very low;

all day long I go about mourning.
My back is filled with searing pain;
   there is no health in my body.
I am feeble and utterly crushed;
   I groan in anguish of heart.

All my longings lie open before you, O LORD;
   my sighing is not hidden from you.
My heart pounds, my strength fails me;
   even the light has gone from my eyes.
My friends and companions avoid me because of
   my wounds;
   my neighbors stay far away.
Those who seek my life set their traps,
   those who would harm me talk of my ruin;
   all day long they plot deception.

I wait for you, O LORD;
   you will answer, O LORD my God.
For I said, "Do not let them gloat
   or exalt themselves over me when my foot
     slips."

O LORD, do not forsake me;
   be not far from me, O my God.
Come quickly to help me,
   O Lord my Savior.
              (1–12, 15–16, 21–22)

Doesn't that sound like the way we feel in the grip of anxiety? Every problem is huge. Doom is sure. Hearts pound. Strength fails. The light goes out of our eyes.

Apparently David was suffering from an acute illness when he wrote this psalm. As so often happens, in the midst of this terrible suffering, two other problems appeared. His friends deserted him (v. 11), and his enemies used the occasion to attack him (vv. 12, 16, 19–20).

Woven throughout the psalm is a thread of anxiety over one central issue. David was greatly troubled not simply because of his physical suffering, not just because his friends deserted him, and not just because his enemies threatened him. His deepest anxiety is revealed in these lines, "My guilt has overwhelmed me like a burden too heavy to bear." He felt vulnerable because of moral failure in his life.

Our lives cannot have stable foundations as long as we carry with us this unsettled inner feeling of guilt. Unfortunately, all of us carry this guilty fear until we specifically deal with our moral failure. We are driven by guilt, and the spiritual vulnerability it brings, until we are made right— justified by faith in Christ.

Stinnette says, ". . . anxiety relentlessly drives man on in his effort to find justification for himself. But peace does not come, as long as anxiety underlies his actions. It comes only as a complete shift of the whole personality from anxiety to faith issues in a quietness and confidence."[3]

Other ways for dealing with this guilty fear have been tried. One method explains away and loosens up the moral values that, when broken, make guilt a reality. We are often tempted to live by adjustable values so that we never need to worry about doing wrong. But that is like saying we will stop talking about and believing in the force of gravity because we're overweight. No matter what we say, we will be affected by gravity. It is a fundamental reality of our existence. In the same way, moral imperatives are fundamental realities that affect our lives whether or not we are willing to recognize them.

The Bible makes no concession to fluid values but maintains that God has revealed his moral will for the human race. That moral will is not open to adjustment. We are to be honest, loving, kind, patient, and holy, among other things, all the time and in every circumstance. When we fail to live up to those standards we are not only guilty, but we injure and are injured.

The answer God offers is not the abolition of moral standards, but absolution of the guilt, and healing for injury. He offers grace as the cornerstone to build a stable life foundation.

The first exchange that must take place to have a stable life foundation is to exchange our guilt for God's grace.

Let me illustrate. Connie was a hardworking mother of three. She was a conscientious person, if anything, overly scrupulous with herself. One Sunday after worship, she knelt at the altar of our church for prayer. As she prayed, tears began to pour down her face.

Her friends gathered around to comfort and pray with her. When she seemed to find little relief, they began asking what was the problem, and how they might help.

Connie told them she felt as though she was falling so far short of being the kind of person God wanted her to be. She was, in fact, wrestling with much the same kind of anxiety David wrote about in the psalm quoted earlier.

Her friends began pointing out her many good qualities and the conscientious way she lived her life. They assured her she was a lovely person and needn't worry about those feelings.

This did little to comfort Connie. Her anxiety remained. Finally, one person moved closer. "Connie," he said, "what's the problem?"

She repeated her story of guilt and anxiety.

After a moment he asked, "Can you think of some specific things you feel guilty about?"

Connie thought for a moment and then spoke hesitantly, "Yes."

"Well, in the Bible, what does God tell us to do with the things we've done wrong?"

Without hesitation Connie answered, "Confess them to him."

"And what does God promise to do if we confess them?"

Connie had stopped crying and her voice was stronger. "He promises to forgive them."

"And if he forgives them, do we need to worry about them?"

"No, I guess not."

"Why not?"

"Well, he forgives them."

"Then, those things you feel guilty about—whether or not they are big or little, or whether you really need to feel guilty about them—maybe you should just confess them to God and ask him to forgive you and take his word that he does."

Connie thought for a moment. Relief came into her face. She bowed her head once more, and with a clear voice prayed for forgiveness. Shortly, she got up from the altar, feeling much better.

Grace means two things. First, there is an infinite reservoir of forgiveness and mercy for all who confess their moral failures and put their lives in God's hands. Second, God promises to be present with us, to accompany us through every step of life, to heal the pain of past injury.

I remember when God began to teach me the limitless depths of his grace. I'm one of those persons who always thinks of how I might have done better. For example, it never did any good for my parents to tell me not to worry about my grades as long as I did my best. I could never do my best, because I could always think of some way I could have done better!

For years, this kept me from understanding and living in the glory of divine grace. My prayers were spent rehearsing all my real and imagined failures, thinking of ways I could have avoided them, begging God to forgive me, but never really feeling that he did.

I had no desire to rebel against God's moral will. I had committed my life to him and tried to live according to his will daily. I held nothing back.

My part of the conversation with God was always anxious, difficult, striving. It was seldom joyful and peaceful.

One year, I went through a period of several months when God seemed to focus my thoughts on the concepts of mercy and grace. As I was meditating about my spiritual life one morning during my devotional time, this sentence came into my head. "God's mercy never runs out."

Suddenly it was as if a brilliant, warm light lit up inside me. For the first time in my life the full meaning of that thought struck me. It was true to Scripture. It had been proven true in other people's lives. God's mercy was demonstrated throughout the Bible.

For a long time I repeated that sentence over and over. God's mercy never runs out. God's mercy never runs out. I saw that we had a living relationship to which we were both committed. That relationship did not depend on performance but on love made possible by his grace and mercy. He loved me. His thoughts were always bent toward me.

This was a turning point in my life—I began to understand the solid foundation God had given me for life.

I learned that grace is the answer for the fear that springs from moral failure. Without grace, we have no solid foundation. Grace is the deepest and most blessed resource we have to conquer fear.

The first exchange is grace for guilt, the second is reverence for pride.

Earlier we discussed two ways of fearing God. I remember my boyhood puzzlement reading the Bible and finding everyone afraid of God. Even the good people "feared" him. In fact, part of the definition of a good person was that he or she was a "God-fearing" person. In one verse you would be exhorted to fear God, and in another you were told to love him. How could you fear something you loved, or love something you feared?

The answer lies in understanding the two kinds of fear. It is significant that in the Bible *fear* is the word most often used to describe the emotions of people in God's presence. It reflects the fact that we can't be indifferent to God. He's not part of the cosmic furniture, nor is he a peer. To be in his presence commands either panic born of guilt, or reverence born of worship.

Reverential fear includes far more than emotion. It includes settled attitudes and willed responses.

Take a look at these verses.

The fear of the LORD is the beginning of knowledge (Prov. 1:7).

The fear of the LORD adds length to life (Prov. 10:27).

He who fears the LORD has a secure fortress (Prov. 14:26).

For those who fear him lack nothing (Ps. 34:9).

The fear of the LORD is pure (Ps. 19:9).

These verses suggest that this fear of God is not negative. It doesn't sound like what we normally think of as fear. The fear of God actually yields confidence. How?

Reverential fear of God is a particular orientation or stance toward him, not just an emotion about him. This relationship with God lifts people to a higher plane of existence, replacing panic with confidence and strength.

Willful pride, which lies at the heart of human nature, stands in the way of reverential fear. Pride always brings us down, just as it did the Israelites time after time. They chose their ways over the ways of God. They trusted their wisdom, strength, and desires, instead of the wisdom and strength of God. God wanted worship and reverence. They gave him arrogance.

When we decide to surrender our lives to God (and it is a surrender), we receive a new orientation. New emotions are made possible. A new inner stability is created.

To exchange pride for reverence is to make God the master of our ways. This reverential fear enables us to look to God for guidance, strength, and hope. Grace forgives our guilt and releases us from the unsettling vulnerability of moral failure; reverence brings daily companionship that inspires, encourages, and directs our lives.

This reverence makes possible an important step in the process of conquering fear. To conquer fear we must face ourselves squarely and honestly. We must come to an awareness of who we are, and what our past has made us. We must own our vulnerabilities. We can't ignore painful things we try to keep buried, those things that (rightly or wrongly) embarrass and frighten us. We have to say, "That's part of me. What can I do about it?" .

Until we have a context in which to be safely vulnerable, we fight these things. We keep our guard up.

When grace and reverence are the context of our lives, we are freed to look deeply at ourselves with the honest, healing gaze of God's love. This allows us to bring whatever we find into his grace. His guidance and companionship will provide answers and solutions. We cannot find a stable foundation without this kind of honesty, healing, and self-acceptance.

Confidence for Timidity

We've identified two exchanges that take place in receiving a stable life foundation. In place of guilty fear, we receive grace. In place of pride, we receive reverence.

These exchanges make possible our daily conversation with God. That conversation gives us a stable foundation, full of confidence in the face of the vulnerabilities of life.

Wise old Solomon said, "In vain you rise early and stay up late, toiling for food to eat—for he grants sleep to those he loves" (Ps. 127:2).

Here's another way to translate those last two lines. "It is vain to eat the bread of anxious toil, because God cares for those he loves, even in their sleep."

Jesus said this in his own way.

Do not worry about your life, what you will eat or drink; or about your body, what you will wear (Matt. 6:25).

Who of you by worrying can add a single hour to his life? (6:27).

Do not worry about tomorrow, for tomorrow will worry about itself (6:34).

How is this done?

Instead of fixing our hearts on the immediate surroundings and outward signs of fear, something fear always demands we do, Jesus told us to fix our minds elsewhere. "You must make God's Kingdom and uprightness before him, your greatest care."[4] It is impossible to think at the same time about the conscious companionship of God and have a hostage-like timidity toward the vulnerabilities of life.

The stable foundation established through grace and reverence gives the assurance of God's daily presence through all of life's experiences.

Gideon might be the patron saint of all cowards. When God found him, he was hiding from his enemies in the bottom of an old cave.

Elijah was a great hero, but he too faced fear. After he

77

defeated the prophets of Baal on Mount Carmel, he went to hide in the desert, fearing for his life.

Moses spent hours in anguish begging God to prevent the enemies of Israel from defeating them.

Joshua marched around Jericho and saw its walls fall down, then sent his men off to conquer Ai. They failed and Joshua went before God with torn clothes and fear in his heart lest their enemies wipe them out.

Israel's greatest leader, David, had his fears. The psalms are full of them.

It would be difficult to find a more flighty, insecure, wrong-headed group of heroes than Jesus' little band of hand-picked disciples.

Yet not one of these people succumbed to fear. There was a kind of stability evident in all their lives. They had found a place to stand when afraid.

Grace must replace guilt.

Reverence must replace pride.

These exchanges make a daily conversation with God possible. That conversation provides the surest, most stable life foundation.

NOTES

[1]Carol Tarvis, "Coping with Anxiety: Treating Mind and Body in America's Number One Health Problem," *Science Digest* (February 1986), 48.

[2]These are not their real names.

[3]Stinnette, p. 123.

[4]Matthew 6:33, *The Complete Bible: An American Translation*. J. M. Powis Smith and Edgar J. Goodspeed, translators (Chicago: University of Chicago Press, 1939).

6

GAINING PERSPECTIVE
THROUGH PRAISE

THE NEED: To conquer fear we need enlarged perspective.

THE RESOURCE: Praise enables us to modify catastrophic mental images and thoughts and thus overcome the tunnel vision that feeds fear.

Laurie slumped in the chair opposite her doctor. Out of desperation she had come to see him for tests. Her recurring symptoms had shaken and baffled her for some time.

One day after her husband left for work and her two children were off to school, a wave of anxiety washed over her. She felt a deep sense of foreboding. Her breathing became jerky and shallow. She felt nauseated.

Her first thought was that something terrible had

happened to her husband or children. The feelings came and went all day, but when her family appeared safely at home that evening, she dismissed the feelings and busied herself with supper.

However, the next morning, when she was once more alone, the same feelings returned. She felt nauseated and shaky; hot flashes surged through her arms and across her chest. These left her almost too weak to work. At the same time, she felt anxious and tense.

On the third day, she woke up dreading being alone, so she made plans to do some shopping as soon as her family left. While shopping, the intense feeling of impending doom swept over her so forcefully that she felt disoriented.

After ten days of these episodes, her hands began to go numb. Laurie decided something must be wrong and made an appointment to see the doctor. She wondered if she was losing her mind, or perhaps had cancer, or heart disease.

The tests showed no abnormalities. Her doctor reassured her that she appeared to be in good physical condition.

Laurie felt desperate. Something was wrong. Was she going crazy? How was she to cope?

Her doctor recommended that she see a therapist. After listening to Laurie describe her physical symptoms, the therapist explained that they were anxiety attacks and asked her to recall the first time she had experienced one. Next, the therapist asked her to describe, as well as she could, the thoughts and mental images that had been going through her mind before and during that episode.

Laurie recalled being tense and worried that first morning. A few days earlier she had spent time with a good friend who lost her husband in an automobile accident. She recalled thinking of how lonely she would be if something like that happened to her family. She remembered replaying scenes in her mind of getting a call from the hospital, of how she would react, of what she would do to hold the family together. Could she keep their home? Would she have to work full-time? What would happen to the children?

The therapist was able to help Laurie establish that before and during her attacks, her mental imagery was always of a particular kind. She had thoughts of something terrible happening to her family and of being left alone. This led her to think about how she would cope with loneliness and grief. Then she felt completely inadequate, and wondered how she would earn a living, pay the bills, and carry on a normal life-style.

Once Laurie was able to see the connection between her mental imagery and anxiety attacks, the therapist had two main tasks. First, Laurie needed to learn how to defuse those mental images before her anxiety got out of hand. By doing so, her physical symptoms eased, though she continued to occasionally worry about her family.

The second task was to try to understand the reasons the thought of being left alone so unnerved Laurie. The therapist asked her to relate any memories or associations that came to her as she relived her anxiety.

One of the associations was remembering the divorce of her parents when she was seven years old. Laurie said, "This reminds me of when my father left. One day he sat down with me and told me he would not be living with me and my mother anymore, but that I would see him now and then. Then he left. It was like he died. Something went out of our home and I didn't think I'd ever be happy again, even though eventually I got over it."

By probing these memories, Laurie was able to see that one of her deepest fears was to lose the emotional security of her family, just as she had when her father left.

81

The Importance of Mental Imagery

Laurie's case illustrates one helpful "discovery" we can make. When we suffer intense anxiety, our minds are preoccupied with mental images. Sometimes these are so routine that they become what therapists call automatic thoughts. They pass through our minds so quickly that we aren't conscious of the thoughts, only the emotions they leave behind.

These thoughts and images can be triggered by a passing word, an event, or a circumstance that reminds us of events or circumstances we find extremely threatening.

The content of these thoughts varies from person to person. Extremely repulsive and frightening ideas may go through our minds repeatedly. We may have images of physical illness or disaster, of doing some violence that horrifies us, of being humiliated in public.

Therapists have found that when people suffer intense anxiety, their minds are saturated with these fearful mental images and automatic thoughts. The spiral of anxiety quickly intensifies when they are unable to deal with them.

Here are the common characteristics of these mental images and automatic thoughts. First, they are images of catastrophe. Our images are of events or circumstances we feel totally unable to handle.

Second, they pass through our minds with all the plausibility and emotional weight of real occurrences. We envision these things *will* happen. They present themselves as images of reality. The thought "What would happen if I got cancer" quickly changes to "I *am* going to get cancer." This sets in motion a whole string of catastrophic consequences.

These images carry the emotional impact of something that has already happened or that is sure to happen, even though part of our mind clearly recognizes that they haven't and that there is no assurance that they will. When these ideas come we are unable to shake the emotional sense that they are real and definitely will happen.

Third, when locked into these images our mental vision possesses an extremely limited scope. Beck and Emery tell of a businessman whose anxiety centered around thoughts of what would happen if his business partner died. He saw himself as being unable to handle the business. The business would deteriorate. He would be bankrupt, and his family would be without support.

His therapists helped him to defuse these fearful images. His anxiety was reduced to manageable levels and he could function normally.

One day the very scenario the man had envisioned did take place. His business partner died. However, instead of the catastrophe he had envisioned, different members of the business pitched in to help pick up the slack, and things carried on as usual.

In his fearful mental imagery, the businessman saw only the bad events and none of the strengths and aids that would help him make it through the disaster.

This is always the case with our fearful mental imagery. We see only the disaster, but none of the helps— the positive circumstances that would get us through the event.

With these points in mind, think about what it's like when your fear alarm goes off. Chances are you will discover that, except in cases where the threat is immediate and physical (like being run over by a car), when you are most anxious your mind is filled with images of disaster.

The Need to Defuse Mental Images

Gaining some sense of realistic perspective on our fearful mental imagery is an important element in dealing with anxiety.

As Laurie's experience illustrates, we do this in two stages. First we defuse the emotional power of the images, then we dig deeper to find out why those particular images bothered us. Instead of spiraling downward into despair and severe anxiety, we take a new mental path that sidesteps the anxiety.

The focus of this chapter is mainly on the first of those two steps. In chapter seven we expand on the second.

Remember, we must first pinpoint the mental imagery that leads us to anxiety, and then begin to consciously modify that imagery.

For example, if our mental imagery is fixed on being spiritually lost, instead of dwelling on our perceived failures and thinking about how terrible it would be to go to hell, we can consciously focus on God's grace and love.[1]

Therapists have many useful tools for helping people with severe anxiety defuse their fearful mental images and automatic thoughts. Some are as simple as breaking the spell with strong sensory input, like clapping your hands sharply several times in succession. Others are more complex and require the interchange of therapist and patient.[2]

The Resource of Praise

What spiritual resource helps us defuse fearful mental images?

The preceding chapters show how our walk with God provides resources to meet specific needs for conquering fear. Does the Bible know anything about the importance of mental imagery?

Consider this verse from Paul. "Finally, brothers, whatever is true, whatever is noble, whatever is right, whatever is pure, whatever is lovely, whatever is admirable—if anything is excellent or praiseworthy—think about such things" (Phil. 4:8).

I always associated this verse with the control of ungodly input, as opposed to righteous input, into my mind. But we can use this verse to test our fearful mental imagery. When catastrophic thoughts come along, we can ask, "At this very moment, is this thought true? Has it already happened? Is it fact, or am I dwelling on a possibility?"

We can set up a grid to examine and modify our mental images with the ideas of this verse. Are the mental images noble? Are they right, pure, lovely, admirable? Can the event, person, or circumstance we are thinking about be constructively helped by thinking about it?

If not, we need to ask how our thoughts deviate from being true, noble, pure, right, and lovely. We must then work to bring those thoughts into line.

The Bible does know about mental imagery. The intent of Paul's verse is to direct the minds of his readers away from useless or destructive mental imagery, toward thoughts that are useful and uplifting.

The next verse says, "Whatever you have learned or received or heard from me, or seen in me—put it into practice. And the God of peace will be with you" (Phil. 4:9).

Peace is what we need and want when we are full of anxiety. We have peace when our mental imagery is occupied with God and his righteousness.

Let's not be unrealistic. Daily life demands our attention to all sorts of things. Few of the thoughts in the forefront of our minds can be about God and his righteousness. Most of us work in secular environments that have little to do with spiritual matters. Everyday activities require most of our attention. How, then, can we defuse our fearful mental images by having minds full of God and his righteousness?

The answer lies in the mental context we set for ourselves. By steeping our minds in God and in the truths of God's Word we set mental tone, just as physical exercise sets muscle tone. *Pre*-occupation with God and his right-eousness brings our memories, mental images, and thoughts into the presence of God. Daily life may demand other considerations. Some may be unpleasant, fearful, and perhaps evil. But *pre*-occupation with God puts a positive image of strength, a point of stability and reference, at the center of our minds.

This may sound mystical but we do it very simply— by worship. Worship issues in praise. Worship and praise are the spiritual resources that help us defuse and modify fearful mental images.

Examples From David

David used praise in connection with his fear. Praise is one of the most characteristic marks of the psalms.

Tradition links the Third Psalm to the time when David's son Absalom staged a coup and forced David to flee from the palace. It was a time of great emotional upheaval. This is what David wrote about it.

> O LORD, how many are my foes!
>   How many rise up against me!
> Many are saying of me,
>   "God will not deliver him."
>
> But you are a shield around me, O LORD,
>   you bestow glory on me and lift up my head.
> To the LORD I cry aloud,
>   and he answers me from his holy hill.
>
> I lie down and sleep;
>   I wake again, because the LORD sustains me.
> I will not fear the tens of thousands
>   drawn up against me on every side.
>
> Arise, O LORD!
> Deliver me, O my God!

Strike all my enemies on the jaw;
break the teeth of the wicked.

From the LORD comes deliverance.
May your blessing be on your people.

Notice that David first pinpoints the threat—in this case the attacks of numerous enemies. No doubt David's enemies seized the opportunity of Absalom's insurrection to attack him. Under normal circumstances they would not have dared.

Second, he runs to the sanctuary of God's presence. "You are a shield around me, O LORD." His immediate choice is to place what threatens him in the context of his relationship with God.

Third, he specifically asks God to intervene and deal with the threat. Fierce, blood-thirsty men sought to kill him. They had no regard for God's anointing David as king of Israel. They were wicked and insensitive to righteousness. "Arise, O LORD! Deliver me, O my God," David cries.

Notice the mental imagery revealed in this psalm. We see that David starts off with a mental image of catastrophe. "O LORD, how many are my foes!" They seemed to overwhelm him.

But David takes steps to modify that imagery or put it into perspective. He affirms that this image of threat concerns people outside the protective shield of God's presence. They can only do to him what God allows. They are also God's enemies. They are wicked people. They must deal with God as well as David.

David introduces ideas that modify his image of himself. He first saw himself as weak, transfixed by the image of enemies with lowered spears charging after him. It's as if he said, "Wait a minute! Who am I? Am I not God's child?"

David broadened the scope of his image to include the

positive helps that would bring him through the circumstance. He rejected the kind of tunnel vision—focusing only on the disaster—that is so common in anxiety.

Finally, he fixed his mind on specific images of victory and peace. "I lie down and sleep; I wake again, because the LORD sustains me. I will not fear the tens of thousands drawn up against me on every side."

What allowed David to reorient his thinking? He began to worship God in the midst of the frightening circumstance.

His worship focused on the nature of God and his relationship with God. The word *praise* is not used but the statements David makes are statements of praise—they are acts of worship.

David ends this psalm with what sounds suspiciously like a caricature of his earlier fearful mental image. "I lie down and sleep; I wake again, because the LORD sustains me. I will not fear the tens of thousands drawn up against me on every side."

This pattern is repeated many times in the psalms. David learned that worship and praise broke the power of the fearful images of disaster and unleashed in his life the power of God to see him through difficult times. Look at this example.

> Keep me safe, O God,
>   for in you I take refuge.
> I said to the LORD, "You are my Lord;
>   apart from you I have no good thing."
> As for the saints who are in the land,
>   they are the glorious ones in whom is all my
>   delight.
> The sorrows of those will increase
>   who run after other gods.
> I will not pour out their libations of blood

or take up their names on my lips.

LORD, you have assigned me my portion and my
    cup;
  you have made my lot secure.
The boundary lines have fallen for me in pleasant
    places;
  surely I have a delightful inheritance.

I will praise the LORD, who counsels me;
  even at night my heart instructs me.
I have set the LORD always before me.
  Because he is at my right hand, I will not be
    shaken.

Therefore my heart is glad and my tongue
    rejoices;
  my body also will rest secure,
because you will not abandon me to the grave,
  nor will you let your Holy One see decay.
You have made known to me the path of life;
  you will fill me with joy in your presence,
  with eternal pleasures at your right hand.
                              (Psalm 16)

Some Points About Praise

The words of Paul and the example of David show
worship and praise as powerful spiritual resources for
defusing and modifying fearful mental imagery.

Many books and sermons stress the necessity to praise
God under all circumstances. Paul's verse has been quoted
to most of us when we least wanted to hear it: "Be joyful
always; pray continually; give thanks in all circumstances,
for this is God's will for you in Christ Jesus" (1 Thess.
5:16–18).

Unfortunately, it is more than just a little difficult to

give thanks and be joyful when it looks like our world is falling apart. How can we be thankful when we're going crazy with anxiety?

It helps to recognize that praise and thankfulness are not the same things. Remember that praise is a function of worship.

When we worship, we do not focus on the events or circumstances around us. We worship God. Our praise, then, is for God, not for circumstances. Circumstances are always secondary.

For example, when we pray for God to meet a financial need and he sends an answer, we praise God for answering prayer. What is the object of our praise? Are we praising the money God has sent? No, we are praising God for having sent the money. The money is the subject of our praise, not its object. The object of praise is God.

Praise does not focus on events or circumstances, but on God who is present in them all.

We always give thanks for *something*. We give thanks for what we appreciate or have received. For example, we thank God for his grace, for good health, for the beauty of the world he has made for us to live in. When we give thanks, our positive feelings are linked to God and the thing about which we give thanks.

It may be possible to sincerely thank God for very unpleasant circumstances. That is difficult, and there is no reason to suppose that God expects us to immediately be thankful *for the fact that we face anxiety or for some terrible event.*

However, we can worship God in the midst of that situation. We can praise him for who he is, for his mercy and loyalty. As we do this, we will be led into thankfulness, perhaps not for the circumstance, but for past victories and positive aspects of our situation. This introduces small but important changes in our mental imagery.

When we praise God, we praise the good we find in him. If we are thankful in all circumstances, it is because we see behind them (by faith) the goodness and faithfulness of God.

In his book, *Conjectures of a Guilty Bystander,* Thomas Merton paraphrases the great medieval mystic, Saint John of the Cross. "Speaking of friendship with Christ, he said that in all friendship there is first a stage at which we see the acts of our friend and come, by them, to know who he is. But after we have come to know who he is, then we see his acts differently, only in the light of *who he is.* Then even acts that would otherwise disconcert us and would seem ambiguous in themselves are accepted because we know who he is. The transition point comes when we know the inmost desires of our friend's heart."[3]

Once we have come to know God, experienced his grace, and come to live in the sanctuary of his presence, we can praise him in all circumstances.

This is not always easy. We should not praise falsely, or simply "because we're supposed to." The important thing is to see why it will not be easy.

It will not be easy because our minds center on the images of impending doom—whether it be spiritual, social, psychological, or physical. Matters that seem more urgent and pressing make us forget the help available to us.

Praise is a powerful resource in helping us to switch images and thoughts. It does not depend on circumstance but on the nature of what we praise. God's nature never changes.

When I praise, my mind shifts from the fearful imagery and thought patterns (those things that seem so real and disastrous) to the grace and goodness of God.

When I worship, I allow myself to be enfolded in the majesty of who God is and of what he makes himself to me.

William James put his finger on our two options.

"There are only two ways in which it is possible to get rid of anger, worry, fear, despair, or other undesirable affections. One is that an opposite affection would break over us, and the other is by getting so exhausted with the struggle that we have to stop—so we drop down, give up, and don't care any longer."[4]

He's right. We can either wallow around in our fearful thoughts, sinking deeper and deeper into anxiety and despair, or we can turn our thoughts toward someone bigger than ourselves.

This life is full of pitfalls and possible disasters. "If we walk at all we walk by faith. Worship is the wellspring of that faith-walking."[5]

Faith-walking—that is the essence of worship, and that is the heart of praise.

Using the Resource of Praise

Bob was a hard worker who reveled in many intense activities. For him the joy of life was in doing constructive work. He hated to be idle.

One day he became ill. He was usually able to shake off illness and keep right on going, but not this illness. He became bedfast, dependent on others to make it through each day. Day after day, week after week, he could do nothing more than lie in bed or hobble to the couch in his living room.

More devastating than the symptoms of physical illness was the anxiety that filled his mind. Was his life finished? Would he ever work again? What would happen to him and his family?

As his anxiety intensified, Bob began to wonder if he was losing his mind. He could not think clearly. The inner spark he always relied on was gone. He felt empty. Things around him seemed unreal. A pall of doom hung over his life.

For a long time, he could scarcely summon the energy to read his Bible and pray. In time he became a bit stronger. He was able to resume some of his work activities. But his anxiety remained. What had happened to him? Would it happen again? Was there something wrong?

The turning point in his healing came one evening as he was reading a Bible story to his children. It was the story of Joseph's being sold into slavery in Egypt. Bob saw what despair Joseph must have felt. Sold into slavery, then sent to prison for something he hadn't done, Joseph lost all he had. However, God used all of those experiences to bring Joseph to a far greater position than he could have ever imagined. Without them, Joseph would have been unprepared.

Later, after his children were asleep, Bob began to praise God. He saw that Paul was right when he said in Romans, God works all things together for the good of his children (8:28). That was just what had happened to Joseph. A new courage began to warm Bob's heart. Into his anxious mind flooded the certainty of God's love even in the midst of the trials and fears he was facing.

Turning to the Eighth chapter of Romans, he read:

Who shall separate us from the love of Christ? Shall trouble or hardship or persecution or famine or nakedness or danger or sword? . . . No, in all these things we are more than conquerors through him who loved us. For I am convinced that neither death nor life, neither angels nor demons, neither the present nor the future, nor any powers, neither height nor depth, nor anything else in all creation, will be able to separate us from the love of God that is in Christ Jesus our Lord (Rom. 8:35, 37–39).

Though his anxieties did not disappear overnight, Bob found new courage as he began to dwell on these truths. His fearful thoughts began to lose their power.

Like Laurie and Bob, we face anxieties. When we do, our minds will be filled with images of catastrophe. Stanley Balwin captured the essence of the spiritual resource we have in praise when he said:

> If I'm to thank God even when the outcome is uncertain, for what shall I give thanks? For past mercies. For His often-demonstrated love. For who He is. As I give thanks for this, my worry is resolved—not by a fantasy that bad things won't happen, but by a realization that if they do, God still lives and will be there with me.[6]

We can be thankful for this, if for nothing else. We worship God because of who he is and in our praise we find our fearful mental images overshadowed by the image of a greater good—the image of One who goes along with us through every twist and turn of life's way.

NOTES

[1]Regardless of how we may *feel* during our times of anxiety, the spiritual reality guaranteed by God's personal revelation is that his grace abounds for all failure and sin. When we confess our sins, God is faithful to forgive them, not once, but as many times as we come to him. Salvation does not lie in us, but in him. In our fearful fantasies of being lost, this reality is obscured by our feeling that somehow *we* are disqualified from God's grace. However, in our lucid moments we can see how blasphemous that thought really is. In fact, if we probe these fearful images of being lost, we may find they have more to do with past

relationships with important figures in our lives than with our relationship with God.

[2]If you would like to know more about these, several books discuss them. The clearest is Beck and Emery's book, *Anxiety Disorders and Phobias: A Cognitive Perspective* (New York: Basic Books, 1985).

[3]Thomas Merton, *Conjectures of a Guilty Bystander* (Garden City, New York: Image Books, 1968), 159.

[4]Stinnette, 112. From William James, *The Varieties of Religious Experience* (New York: The Modern Library, 1929), 208.

[5]Stinnette, 156.

[6]Stanley Balwin, "Don't Worry is Bad Advice," *Moody Monthly* (July 1985), 63.

7

FINDING HOPE IN PERSONAL HISTORY

THE NEED: To conquer fear we need hope.

THE RESOURCE: By tracing the footprints of God through our history, our hope for the future is renewed.

Okonkwo was a man of action, tall, burly, sure of voice and manner. He lived during the time of upheaval when European missionaries and traders first began to explore his Ibo tribal area in Nigeria.

At the center of Okonkwo's life was a powerful contradiction. Though he was a man of action, a respected leader among his people, he was held hostage by fears with roots that went deep into his past.

Okonkwo learned early in life that his father, Unoka, was a dreamer. Unoka preferred to sit at the door of his hut, playing his flute and dreamily reflecting on a private world. He was a gentle man who reveled in beautiful things but was unable to provide for his family.

Unoka lived serenely in debt to others in his village. His gardens never flourished. This caused untold hardship for his family. It never bothered Unoka. He was content to go through life on his own terms.

Okonkwo never forgave him for this. The shame that should have been Unoka's, Okonkwo felt deeply and took upon himself. The hardship brought on by his father's lackadaisical life bit deeply into his young body and mind. He made up his mind early that he would be everything his father had not been. He would show everyone what he could become, despite his father's shameful condition.

As a result, Okonkwo's "whole life was dominated by fear, the fear of failure and of weakness. . . . It was the fear of himself, lest he should be found to resemble his father. . . . even now he still remembered how he had suffered when a playmate had told him that his father was *agbala* (an old woman). . . . And so Okonkwo was ruled by one passion—to hate everything that his father Unoka had loved. One of those things was gentleness and another was idleness."[1]

The fear at the center of his life took its toll in many ways, but Okonkwo never realized the lengths to which it would drive him.

In Ibo culture of that period, an offense by one village against another could be redressed in two ways. The wronged village could go to war to defend itself. But since war was costly for both sides, it was avoided if at all possible.

To avoid war, the offending village could send one of its people, chosen by lot or by the elders, to live in the offended village. Vengeance could then be symbolically taken on that person as the village desired. Sometimes this person was killed. Other times he or she was allowed to become a member of a household within the village.

One day a man from a neighboring village killed one of the people of Okonkwo's village. Rather than face the prospect of war with Okonkwo's village, well-known as fierce and powerful warriors, the village elders chose by lot one of the murderer's youngest sons and sent the child to Okonkwo's village as a peace offering.

After some debate, the village elders decided not to kill the child for the time being and sent him to live in Okonkwo's household.

At first the boy cried all the time for his mother, but in time he came to accept his new surroundings. He never understood what had happened, because he was so young, but as the months and years passed he came to love Okonkwo and to call him Father. In turn, Okonkwo came to love the boy even more than his own son.

One day the village deity declared to the elders that the child must be killed to avenge the wrong done to their village. None of them relished the task, but they made plans to carry out the sentence.

When a wise old neighbor heard this decree, he went to Okonkwo's home with some advice. "A child should never be killed by him whom he calls Father. Take no part in the killing. Let the other men of the village carry out the decree. No one will blame you for not accompanying the men into the forest."

With heavy heart, Okonkwo wrestled with this problem. He loved the boy as his own son and could not bear the thought of his being killed. But deep in his heart, the old fear held him hostage. More than anything, he feared being called *agbala*.

The day the sentence was to be carried out, Okonkwo told the boy he could accompany the village men into the forest on a hunting trip. Filled with excitement the boy set out with them, walking single file along the path through the leafy, chirruping forest. As he walked, he began to sense something amiss. The faces of the men were not quite right.

He began to feel frightened. As the fear spread through his mind, the boy turned to look behind him. There he saw Okonkwo swinging along, big, steady, and powerful as always. Relief flooded over him. His father would let nothing harm him.

Meanwhile, the struggle was raging in Okonkwo. There was no reason for him to take part in carrying out this sentence. No one would blame him for going home. But every time he made up his mind to turn back, that old gnawing fear would rise up and he would keep going.

He could take the struggle no more. At last it was time for the sentence to be fulfilled. Summoning his strength, with deep loathing in his heart, he called the boy's name. The boy turned to face him with questioning eyes.

In that instant, Okonkwo's big knife flashed down, taking the boy's life.

In shame at what he had done, Okonkwo turned and fled for his hut, where he stayed for many days.

Life never would be the same. Not only was his life dominated by his old fear, it was now dominated by self-loathing as well. According to their laws the sentence had to be carried out, but Okonkwo's neighbors came to despise him for what he had done.

Dealing Redemptively With Our Personal Histories

This story is told by the great Nigerian writer, Chinua Achebe, in his novel *Things Fall Apart*. Okonkwo lives the rest of his life trying to prove his strength to himself and his neighbors. Driven by his fears, unable to come to terms with his past, Okonkwo sinks deeper into tragedy.

The story illustrates two important facts about anxieties. First, we can almost always trace them to origins in our own personal history. Second, we are doomed to wrestle with them until we deal redemptively with our history.

We face daily life out of a certain mental context that is ours alone.[2] Sometimes this is called our worldview, though that term usually connotes political and religious values. Therapists call this mental context our cognitive set.

This cognitive set is uniquely ours because it is a product of our personal history—the experiences we have had throughout life, the influences and the responses we have made along the way.

This mental context or cognitive set guides the way we interpret and respond to life events. Therapists have discovered that they can discern general themes as they work through the process of collecting and defining a patient's mental images and automatic thoughts—the images around which anxieties center. With these themes they can begin to outline the patient's cognitive set. In turn these themes lead to an understanding of the basic concerns of the patient's anxieties.

All of us have one or more basic concerns that dominate our inner life. Okonkwo's basic concerns were to avoid weakness and failure. He feared any circumstance that made him feel weak or like a failure. Based on these concerns, he assumed that he could never show weakness of any kind. His assumption was that constant activity, material success, and outward bravado would protect him against his major concerns. This grew out of his personal history—his experiences as a child with his father.

Clearly facing our basic concerns gives us the chance to work with our anxiety objectively, to challenge our assumptions, and to free ourselves to develop more realistic and positive approaches to life.

Our basic concerns usually follow patterns throughout our life. Our anxieties often revolve around one or two central issues. Events or circumstances that impinge on those central issues trigger our anxiety.

For example, people who lived through the Great Depression often decry the throw-away values of the "baby boom" generation. Their cognitive set was formed with experiences that taught them the fragility of wealth, the ease with which it can disappear, and the hardship of life in poverty. For them, anxiety might center on losing material assets like a home or land. They face life with a certain mental context and interpret life from that context.

Many people have a concern for the emotional security derived from personal relationships. These people often live with the assumption that confrontation or conflict within relationships means risking emotional security. They live in fear of conflict and need constant assurances of love.

Some conflict is inevitable in personal relationships and need not lead to separation and emotional insecurity. Conflict can be used to make a relationship better. Until these people examine the roots of their anxiety about interpersonal conflict and reform their false assumptions, they will be pursuing crippling approaches to personal relationships.

Conquering anxiety requires clarifying and dealing with our basic concerns and assumptions. In order to do that, we need to explore our personal history.

In the last chapter we saw that to conquer fear we need to defuse the emotional power of our catastrophic mental images. But equally important is the analysis I've outlined here. We must come to terms with concerns that control our catastrophic mental imagery.

Another great spiritual resource comes into play at this point. What can we do with our past? Do we explain it away or try to forget it? What perspective should we have in exploring our personal history?

One of the great joys of our walk with God is using the past redemptively. We don't need to cover up the painful, shameful past or attempt the unrealistic task of forgetting it. We don't discount it or explain it away. Instead we learn from it.

Stinnette put his finger on the resource God gives us for dealing redemptively with our past.

> The tragedy of much of the "self-help" literature of this age is that it covers with a thin veneer the treacherous break-throughs in man's inner-life, which, if taken more seriously as opportunities for self-knowledge, could lead to profound renewal rather than to bitter frustration. For all its confidence, Christianity is not a grand detour around suffering, but a highway through the "valley" and the "shadow" to the presence of God.[3]

Finding God In Our Past

David's life is a wonderful example of the perspective we need because his approach to life took in the present, the future, and the past. He saw his present life and future possibilities within the context of a past he had shared with God.

We have the spiritual resource of seeing our past in the light of God's presence in it. This gives us hope in facing threatening events and circumstances in the present and the future.

As we review our personal history, we see more than our own footsteps through time. We see God moving through that history with us. Until we look at life from this perspective, we miss the telltale signs of his grace at every turn.

Our history is full of grace, just as our future is full of grace. We can see grace in our future because we can see it in our past. When we search our history as children of God, we search a history shared with God.

This was one of David's greatest sources of hope. No matter what plagued him, he seemed to have a bottomless well (within his cognitive set) of living hope. He had his moments of despair and fear, as reflected in many psalms. But he had hope. His mental context was not dominated by catastrophe or despair.

Here is an example of the way David viewed his present difficulties in the light of God's presence in his past.

> To you, O LORD, I lift up my soul;
>   in you I trust, O my God.
> Do not let me be put to shame,
>   nor let my enemies triumph over me.
> No one whose hope is in you
>   will ever be put to shame,
> but they will be put to shame
>   who are treacherous without excuse.
>
> Show me your ways, O LORD,
>   teach me your paths;
> guide me in your truth and teach me,
>   for you are God my Savior,
>   and my hope is in you all day long.
> Remember, O LORD, your great mercy and love,
>   for they are from of old.
> Remember not the sins of my youth
>   and my rebellious ways;
> according to your love remember me,
>   for you are good, O LORD.
>
> Good and upright is the LORD;
>   therefore he instructs sinners in his ways.
> He guides the humble in what is right
>   and teaches them his way.

All the ways of the LORD are loving and faithful
  for those who keep the demands of his
      covenant.
For the sake of your name, O LORD,
  forgive my iniquity, though it is great.
Who, then, is the man that fears the LORD?
  He will instruct him in the way chosen for
      him.
He will spend his days in prosperity,
  and his descendants will inherit the land.
The LORD confides in those who fear him;
  he makes his covenant known to them.
My eyes are ever on the LORD,
  for only he will release my feet from the snare.
Turn to me and be gracious to me,
  for I am lonely and afflicted.
The troubles of my heart have multiplied;
  free me from my anguish.
Look upon my affliction and my distress
  and take away all my sins.
See how my enemies have increased
  and how fiercely they hate me!
Guard my life and rescue me;
  let me not be put to shame,
  for I take refuge in you.
May integrity and uprightness protect me,
  because my hope is in you.

Redeem Israel, O God,
  from all their troubles!

(Psalm 25)

David begins and ends practicing the choice we talked
about earlier. He turns directly to God for sanctuary and
refuge. Throughout the prayer, he recognizes that God's

help comes to those willing to walk in God's ways, who are persons of integrity and uprightness.

Woven throughout this psalm is an affirmation of the faithfulness of God. David knows about this faithfulness, because he knows God's mercy and love "from of old." He recites a litany of God's faithfulness. He guides and instructs the humble. His ways are loving and faithful for those who keep covenant with God. As we read these words, we sense David tracing the presence of God back through his own history, and the history of godly persons he has known. This gives David hope that God will act the same way in his present difficulties.

We can also trace the grace of God in our lives. He has been present in our lives and in the lives of godly people we know.

Hope for the future based on the knowledge of the past—this spiritual resource is ours. Here is another example of David's affirmation of God's presence in his history.

> I waited patiently for the LORD;
>> he turned to me and heard my cry.
> He lifted me out of the slimy pit,
>> out of the mud and mire;
> he set my feet on a rock
>> and gave me a firm place to stand.
> He put a new song in my mouth,
>> a hymn of praise to our God.
> Many will see and fear
>> and put their trust in the LORD.
>
> Blessed is the man
>> who makes the LORD his trust,
> who does not look to the proud,
>> to those who turn aside to false gods.
> Many, O LORD my God,

are the wonders you have done.
The things you planned for us
no one can recount to you;
were I to speak and tell of them,
they would be too many to declare.
(Psalm 40:1–5)

As with Psalm 25, David ends with a plea for God to help him out of his fearful circumstances. We see that David's mental context is characterized by hope that is drawn from the affirmation of God's presence in his own personal history. David can face fearful circumstances partly because he knows God has been present with him in past difficulties. It is God's nature to help him, and God's nature doesn't change.

David's hope was not just wishful thinking. He could point to instance after instance in his own history when God had taken him through hard times.

We find hope for our present as we affirm God's presence in our past. We need to face life's fearful events and circumstances with this kind of assumption.

Coming to Terms With Our Basic Concerns

In Achebe's story, Okonkwo's anxieties centered on two basic concerns—being a "failure," and being tagged a weak person. These anxieties were historically tied to the shame and hardship he blamed on his father. Though they were shaped and modified through the years by Okonkwo's personality and by his choices, they had their roots in his past experiences.

Therapists often lead patients through a series of steps to help them come to grips with the sources of their anxieties. One common way of doing this was introduced in chapter six.

The patient is asked to tell (or to make a written

record of) all the associations and memories that come to mind while in the grip of anxiety. The patient will often recall instances from childhood, or some other period in life, that directly relate to his or her issues of anxiety.

The therapist explores the patient's history by asking probing questions, clarifying the issue at stake in the person's anxiety, and encouraging the individual to sort through the events and forces that have resulted in his or her life situation.

As we ask the question "What events and circumstances in my personal history have made this particular issue one that brings me anxiety?" an exploration of our past takes place.

Remember two main ideas. First, our cognitive set is made up of four kinds of data—feelings, thoughts, assumptions, and issues. Feeling is the most immediate of these, the one about which we are most aware. We have mental feelings and physical feelings. These are always tied to thoughts (mental images and automatic thoughts), which are tied to our assumptions, and grow out of basic issues or concerns at the root of our personality.

In the process of exploring our personal history we move through these various kinds of data, always driving at the most basic level. We want to arrive at an understanding of the concerns and issues most basic to our cognitive set. Then we can modify assumptions and exercise better judgment about our thoughts and feelings.

Second, anxiety is our mind's alarm system to tell us of something it interprets to be dangerous. That danger may be spiritual, emotional, social, or physical. We identify that particular event or circumstance with danger in one or more of these areas.

How? Some fears seem to be innate (such as fears of snakes and heights), but most things that appear dangerous have been learned through personal experience. We have encountered them in the past, and that encounter has taught us to beware of them in the future.

It's easy to see why fear is such a complex problem. Anything can cause anxiety as long as it is associated with danger. Reality or fiction, rationality or irrationality, have little to do with the issue. Whether the threat is "real" or not, the interpretation of threat is very real, so our anxiety is very real.

In the last chapter we saw that to carry on when anxiety comes we must defuse the emotional power of the interpretation. But this alone will never free us from the tyranny of those fears.

One necessary key to conquering fear is being able to relate our anxiety to the basic concerns that were formed through the experiences of our past.

What do we do with these basic issues once we have identified them?

First, just knowing anxiety is understandable within the context of our personal history helps take away its power to tyrannize our present and future.

Second, we need to see that we have the power to choose what to do with our basic concerns. We have developed, perhaps over many years, habits of thought based on faulty assumptions. These habits of thought are so well ingrained in us, they may seem inevitable. They appear to have a life of their own. But they do not. Just as habits were formed through repetition, they can be reformed through repetition.

Let me share with you, not without a sense of vulnerability, one of my most basic concerns, to which my anxiety is often tied. It was at the root of many fears in Haiti, and has plagued me throughout my adult life. I have a fear of being homeless and alone.

For all of my marriage I have had a recurring nightmare. During the first five years it would recur many times a month. It comes with less frequency these days.

The common theme of these nightmares is that I will be separated from my wife and children. I would wake up in a cold sweat, with my heart in my throat, enveloped in a sense of dread.

I traveled a lot during the first year I returned to the States from Haiti, speaking to different groups about our ministry. I cannot begin to recount the many times that year I would lie in a strange room with heart pounding, gripped by a sense of despair and anxiety. I don't know how many times I spent the hours driving home wrestling with the "certainty" that my wife and family would be gone when I got home. The feelings were very real. Telling myself this fear was "irrational" did no good.

The life-style of my missionary parents and my own life-style have meant that I have no "homeplace." I have averaged a move about every other year my entire life. Sometimes I cannot bear to think about the future, because doing so brings me this same sense of impending doom and dread, of being lost and alone in a world in which I have no place.

These are some of my strongest anxieties. My personal history sheds much light on them. In my heart is a deep longing for a place to put down roots, a place where I can belong.

My feelings of dread and insecurity are like those I recall having as a child in certain piercing memories that are as real as if they happened yesterday.

When I was perhaps three years old, we were living in Manila for a short period, in a narrow, three-story row house made of cement block. On one occasion my parents needed to attend a meeting so they left me with a sitter. We were alone in the house and I can remember feeling terrified at having been left there. To make matters worse, my sitter went to the basement where there was a shower room. There she closed the door and began to shower. To this day, I can see that dark basement with its stark concrete walls, and recall my panic and dread at being alone. Screaming hysterically I beat and beat on the door.

There were other similar occasions. Once my parents left my sister and me with sitters and went to a village several hours away from our house to hold weekend meetings. I can still see the scene of my parents driving away as clearly as if it happened yesterday. The feelings come back just as clearly. I almost went crazy with panic. I felt utterly alone, hopeless, and desperate as they drove away.

The most intense experience came when I had to go away to boarding school. The school was one for missionary children. It was a wonderful place and I recall many things about it with fondness. But my childhood ended the day I left for school.

I was about ten years old. My first semester was spent with another missionary family. The next semester I moved into a dorm on campus. After all these years I still cannot recall those days without great anguish. I felt so alone, vulnerable, lost.

Perhaps the worst memories were the times I would have to return to school after Christmas, or summer vacation. I knew I must go, but did not want to go. I felt such despair.

As I have examined these anxieties, I remember personal experiences that have taught me that being separated from those I love, from my emotional "nest," is a terrible experience. One of my life's basic concerns has been to maintain a sense of emotional security by keeping closely attached to people I love.

What do I do with these experiences from my past? How do I deal with my past?

111

I will never forget the light that dawned when I saw one key point about those memories. Those experiences were painful and left their mark on me, but I do not have to remain hostage to them. They are in my past. I can't deny them, explain them away, or forget them. But I am free to choose how I will respond to them in the present.

I've had many years of practice living on assumptions formed by those experiences. It would be foolish to suppose I can immediately overcome that practice.

But the process of dealing redemptively with my past has enabled me to see that I can choose how to interpret those painful events that formed my basic concerns. When my parents left me, they always came back. I have struggled with resentment that they would send me away from home, but I can also choose to dwell on the fact that they did it because they thought it was best for me, not out of negligence or lack of love. As an adult, I don't have to agree with their decision to see that it was motivated by love.

To live my life with catastrophic assumptions based on experiences is to remain hostage to a single way of viewing them. Instead I can choose to see that even in those events, I was not lost, and I am not lost now.

I can choose to modify the assumptions that grow out of my basic concerns.

Third, the greatest strength we can find is in taking the conscious step of looking for, and reaffirming the presence of God in our past. Just as David was able to point to the footsteps of God through his history, our hearts fill with hope and joy as we see God's footprints through our past.

What do I mean? For one thing, God has this way of turning painful events into useful ones. I learned a very great deal from the experience of going away from home. It has put certain other strengths into my character that might not have been there otherwise. As I face the basic concerns of my life (and the one I've shared here is only one of them), I can find positive results God has brought out of disastrous circumstances.

I don't revel in the painful past, but I am thankful for the good God has brought out of bad. That's one aspect of the grace of God in our personal history.

Another is to see how God has all along given us just what we have needed as we relied on him. Though there is no physical space I can call my homeplace, I belong to a large and close-knit family. At our family reunions there is no bickering, fighting, or jealousy. We enjoy each other. My own immediate family is a haven of happiness and security. Everywhere I have gone, I've found friends. God's grace has given me many wonderful things to be thankful for.

You can do the same in your life. Begin by facing your own history and identifying any evidences of grace. Reaffirm these. God is always present in your life with grace and strength. Make that truth a base assumption of your mental context. Then you will have new hope to face the present and the future.

I began this chapter with a story of tragedy. Okonkwo never came to terms with his past, so his life was lived under the tyranny of his fears. I'd like to finish with a story of hope and victory.

Augustine was one of the greatest figures in the history of the Christian church. His work has influenced countless individuals from his day to the present.

The story of his life is fascinating. Indulged as a child, wild and willful as a young man, he was nevertheless beset with great anxiety. He had a horror of being lost. He seemed to feel as though he were suspended by a hair over a great chasm of despair. The conscious longing of his life was for peace and safety.

Then something happened. During one period of

Augustine's life, God's grace reached through to him. His conversion was deep and lasting. Though he often regretted his past, he was able to come to terms with it, to shake off the tyrannical shackles of his own history.

In the end, this was said of his life.

> Augustine was not a placid man nor a faultless one nor exempt from acute (anxiety). His childhood was unhealthy; his adolescence neurotic. His mature life was spent in a demoralized world and he died in an uproar, with the Vandals battering at the walls of Hippo. His conscious longing was for "peace" but he found precious little of it in his outward circumstances. Yet this same man ... lived and died with an inner steadiness and productivity, as if he had found his rest on bedrock, beneath life's heaving surfaces. He had found a "cure" for his ... anxiety and this made all the difference.[4]

Just as Augustine, we have the privilege of tracing through our own history the legacy of God's grace. God has been with us in the past, and he is with us now to heal and to remake us. The hope that comes as we trace the footprints of God through our past and into our present is one of the most precious spiritual resources we have for conquering fear.

NOTES

[1]Chinua Achebe, *Things Fall Apart* (Greenwich, Conn.: Fawcett Publications, 1959), 16–17.

[2]I am indebted, once again, to Beck and Emery for the discussion that follows. While this line of thinking is not unique to them, their discussion of this subject is the best I have found.

[3]Stinnette, *Anxiety and Fear*, 92.

[4]Hiltner, "Theories of Anxiety," 95.

8
FINDING COMFORT IN
THE COMMUNITY
OF FAITH

THE NEED: To conquer fear we need the solace of nurturing relationships.

THE RESOURCE: The community of faith provides a
network of relationships marked by
trust, acceptance, and reassurance.

Soeur[1] Marie's wizened old face peered into the open
door of my office. Tentatively, yet with that challenging air
that was all her own, she cleared her throat. "Pastor David,
I must talk to you. You're always busy, I know, but I must
talk to you."

Soeur Marie had been around the campus at Petit
Goave since long before I was born. It was her place. In past
years she had done various jobs for missionaries. She
proudly enjoyed lecturing me about the many good deeds

she had done. She had held Sunday school classes and visited churches with the pastors and missionaries.

But the years had taken their toll on Soeur Marie. When I came to know her, she was an old woman, poor in every way, physically unattractive, and pugnacious of manner.

Most of my encounters with Soeur Marie centered around her demands for food, clothing, or money, and for work for her adult son. At first my wife and I did what we could, but when she came more often with more strident demands, we found ourselves at a loss. When we refused her demands, she complained loudly and sometimes belligerently.

One day after my wife turned down one of her requests Soeur Marie protested. "Now if Jesus was here," she said, "and I came to him and asked for something, he would not turn me away. And you are supposed to be his representative here. How can you claim to represent Jesus and still turn me away?"

Though I am not proud to say so, Soeur Marie and I did not become fast friends. I avoided her as often as possible. I knew her life was difficult, and I wanted to help her. But there were limits to what I could do. As my help was met by more forceful demands, I found it difficult to have patience and compassion. At least, that's how I excused myself.

But there she was glowering at me as usual. "Pastor David, I've got to talk to you."

With a sigh I asked, "Oh, is that right?" I expected the usual list of demands.

"Yes. You're always too busy to talk to me, but I must see you."

I resigned myself to another harangue and said, "Well, okay. But I really am busy right now. If you come to my house this evening we will talk." With disgust, she agreed and went on her way.

I was cleaning the dishes that evening when Soeur Marie knocked on my back door. The evening brought some respite from the day's heat, so the most pleasant place to sit was on the small patio behind my house. Scarcely before we were seated, she began.

"Pastor David, I had a dream the other night. In my dream, one of the old missionaries asked me why I had never come to pray with you. I told him I had not come because you never have time for me. But he reminded me I had always prayed with the other missionaries. I should pray with you, too. So that's why I'm here. We are going to pray."

Soeur Marie began a long rambling talk, much of which I could not decipher. But as she talked I began to pick up the drift of her thoughts.

She told of the many threatening circumstances of her life. She told me about her fears for herself and her son, who refused to follow God. She talked of how she often had very little to eat, and how even so, she shared what she had with her son so he could work to feed his children. Then she told me of how, in spite of her fears, she drew comfort and strength from God's presence.

Then she turned to me and said, "Pastor David, I know you are a young man. I know you have a very hard job to do here. And I know you often do not know what you should do. But I want to encourage you. God will not abandon you. You just keep doing what you know to do. God will be with you. Keep up your courage."

Then, abruptly, she said, "Now we are going to pray. I will pray and you give the benediction." She bowed her head and began to pray for me in her confusing Creole.

As I listened to Soeur Marie, my heart was both chastened and uplifted. My work was very difficult. I often wondered how to respond to the many demands of our ministry, just as she had said. So how did God choose to send encouragement? By the presence of this poor, pugnacious old saint praying for me.

As I've reflected on the significance of Soeur Marie's visit I've been reminded of the process of making movies. Two sets of people appear in movies. There are the stars—the important people, the people with power to make the movie succeed or fail. They are admired. Their every wish is met.

Then there are the extras. Extras aren't worth much. They have no power. Their wishes aren't consulted. They are just there, part of the scenery.

By every human assessment, Soeur Marie was an extra. She had no power. She was important to very few people. Most of the time, she was someone I wanted to avoid. As I thought of the encouragement she gave me, and her prayer for me, it was as though God said, "In my world, there are no extras." We all matter to God. And so we are all of worth to each other.

God used a wizened little old Haitian lady to share his love with me. In the process I saw beyond the superficial traits I had found so difficult to accept. I caught a glimpse of the true worth of Soeur Marie and of others like her. In so doing I saw something I hope to never forget.

Some of our greatest spiritual resources for conquering life's threatening circumstances are found in the fellowship of the community of faith.

A Network of Nurturing Relationships

In the last four chapters we've discussed several important elements needed in order to conquer anxiety. We've also discussed the resources our spiritual life makes available for these elements.

We need a place of sanctuary to retreat to for renewed

courage. This is provided when we enter God's presence by faith and obedience.

We need a stable life foundation. This is provided when we exchange guilt for grace, and pride for reverence.

We need to defuse the emotional power of our catastrophic mental images, and to expand the limited vision they bring. This is provided by praise and worship.

In the previous chapter we saw that we must come to terms with the basic concerns and assumptions that control our anxiety. This happens when we deal redemptively with our personal history.

In this chapter we will discuss a final element, one that is illustrated by my encounter with Soeur Marie. We need a network of positive, nurturing personal relationships.

The lesson I learned from Soeur Marie has been repeated for me over and over. So often when I've needed a lift, a friend or family member who shares my faith has given me the solace of his or her presence and love, and the encouragement of shared prayer.

One of the fundamental ways therapy helps people is by providing a positive, nurturing relationship between the therapist and the patient.

Just as there are spiritual resources to meet our needs for sanctuary, hope, healing, and courage, there is a spiritual resource to help meet this need for nurturing relationships. To develop these loving relationships we have the community of faith.

Self-worth and Interpersonal Relationships

The community of faith provides two resources that address closely related issues—our sense of self-worth and our interrelationships.

Being a part of the community of faith provides a healthy way of viewing our self-worth. This, coupled with the values inherent to the community of faith, puts relationships in the context of shared respect, mutual trust, and active love.

What I've just stated is the ideal. In fact, we often go on living in the community of faith with values and self-concepts foreign to it. In addition, not all relationships within the community will have the same level of intimacy. However, there are few other contexts in which such closeness and nurture are possible. The body of Christ is to be a community in which we share one another's burdens. If it is less than that, it is not truly the body of Christ.

Robert Frost's poem, "Revelation," reminds us of our need for nurturing human friendships. He recognizes that instead of reaching out, we often hide ourselves away. Not only do we fear our fears, but we fear the loss of respect we think will follow if we share them. As a result we make ourselves places apart and needlessly suffer alone. We hide heavy hearts behind light words when we need friends to lift the load with us.

> We make ourselves a place apart
>   Behind light words that tease and flout,
> But oh, the agitated heart
>   Till someone find us really out.
>
> Tis pity if the case require
>   (Or so we say) that in the end
> We speak the literal to inspire
>   The understanding of a friend.
>
> But so with all, from babes that play
>   At hide-and-seek to God afar.
> So all who hide too well away
>   Must speak and tell us where they are.[2]

We need to put away games of hide-and-seek when in the grip of anxiety. We need to share honestly, without shame, and receive honest comfort and encouragement in return.

Some Common Basic Concerns That Trigger Anxiety

Let's delve a little deeper into the reasons for the importance of nurturing personal relationships for the purpose of conquering fear.

Researchers have found three very common basic concerns in our society. They are acceptance, competence, and control. Let's look at what these mean.

If our basic concern is acceptance, we crave the emotional security provided by the approval of others. As a result, we fear personal conflict. We go to great lengths to earn the acceptance of those around us. If we are left out, even unintentionally, we are devastated. Life becomes a story of domination, because we are unwilling to risk disapproval.

If our basic concern is competence, we fear being labeled a failure. Our senses of worth and meaning come from recognized achievement. We need to prove to ourselves and to others that we're on top of everything. We cannot be vulnerable. We fear being embarrassed. We drive ourselves mercilessly and put up false fronts of smooth bravado.

If our concern is control, we fear being dominated by someone else, or by outward circumstances. We refuse to risk intimacy because we fear the control it might bring. Even though we may go along outwardly, inwardly we are wary of giving in to rules and authority. We become islands of fastness, isolated from those around us.

In thinking about these three common basic concerns, a couple of themes emerge. First, they all have to do with our self-concept and the way it impacts our interpersonal relationships. Second, there is a faulty self-concept that leads to broken, unrealistic, or unhealthy relationships in all three cases.

Why are these basic concerns so common in our society? What is it that gives us such difficulty with the important issues of self-worth and interpersonal relationships?

We often have anxiety over acceptance, competence, and control because of some central ideas that shape our thinking about these issues in our modern Western culture. We gain insight into this question by considering one of the central characteristics of our culture.

Competitive Individualism

A wealth of literature from both Christian and non-Christian writers reveals that in our modern Western culture the worth and meaning of human life is decided according to the value of "competitive individualism."

Rollo May put it this way. "Individual competitive success is both the dominant goal in our culture and the most pervasive occasion for anxiety."[3]

Competitive individualism, along with many other values that undergird our present culture, came to prominence during a particular period of Western European history known as the Renaissance. This period, from the fourteenth through the seventeenth centuries, was one of tremendous intellectual and artistic change within Western European culture.

Before the Renaissance, during the Middle Ages, personal worth and meaning were governed by one's social status at birth. If you were born to royalty, your life took on a certain meaning and worth. If you were born of common blood, your life had a different, though just as real, meaning and worth. These questions, as well as the accepted rules for personal interaction, were governed by a stable social organization. Everyone knew their place and knew what was expected. There was widespread agreement on the moral and ethical rules that shaped society. In short, the community gave meaning to the individual. This did not mean people of that time had no anxieties. Life was often filled with difficulty and hardship. It simply meant anxieties were of a different kind.

By the fourteenth and fifteenth centuries, this form of social organization had grown so rigid and top-heavy that ordinary people were at its mercy. The needs and rights of common people began to suffer under the demands of the rigid social hierarchy. This was reflected in the high incidence of depression, melancholy, skepticism, and anxiety. People's anxieties revolved around death, devils, and sorcery. They felt helpless beneath the overwhelming social power of royalty and other authorities. Their fears were of forces that seemed mysterious, beyond their control.

During the Renaissance a reaction took place against this top-heavy society. One of its major features was the enormous emphasis put on individual achievement. Remember that during the Middle Ages, the worth and meaning of individual persons was defined in the context of the community into which they were born. With the Renaissance, however, the community, rather than defining the worth and meaning of individual lives, became a backdrop against which the individual was, *by personal achievement*, to prove his or her worth and meaning.[4]

This new view set the stage for the scientific and artistic achievements of the seventeenth century. It pushed people to create new ideas, new art, and pursue new scientific breakthroughs. But it also carried the seeds of the anxieties we now face.

To reiterate, during the Middle Ages the meaning and worth of human life were established at birth by fate, or by the will of God, according to one's membership in the community. Whether of royal or common blood, every person had his or her place.

The Renaissance introduced the idea that the value and meaning of a human life was not necessarily given at birth but was defined by the person's individual achievements. The legacy of this idea can be found in some of the clichés we hear today. You must live up to your potential, create a niche for yourself, make your own way in the world.

Out of this view grew the competitive individualism of today. It is individualism because the emphasis is no longer on the community but on the individual. It is competitive because the individual must compete with other individuals for place and achievement to establish his or her worth.

The result is that human life tends to lose its intrinsic value. Our respect and regard for each other becomes based on achievement, rather than on the mere fact of being human.

For example, we admire those who by dedication and skill have reached the top of their sport. Many are minorities who come from poor and disadvantaged backgrounds. The unfortunate reality is that it doesn't seem strange to us that we would have no admiration, no regard for them if they had remained in the ghetto, or on welfare. Instead, this seems a natural state of affairs. People are respected, not because they are human beings, but because they are humans beings who achieve, who get ahead.

We hope things would be different in the church, but we seem to be drawn more to those who build huge "ministries" with glittering buildings and fancy programs than to faithful servants who know parishioners by name and give their lives to quiet, steady service.

Business executives who increase the bottom-line profits of companies and pay stockholders higher dividends are rewarded even if they destroy people's jobs and swindle customers in the process. Corporate takeovers and leveraged buy-outs leave many faithful company employees without jobs, but those who pull them off are respected.

The worth of a working person becomes reduced to the number of parts he or she can turn out in a day and the number of days worked without injury or sick leave.

In our society, the worth and meaning of human life have come to be defined by personal achievement instead of by the fact of being human. Is it any wonder our sense of self-worth goes awry when as a society we have a perilous way of thinking about the worth and meaning of human life.

We live in isolation, without any sense of community, at least partly because our social forms promote individualism and competition. This mind-set contributes to personal relationships that are often broken and unhealthy.

The ultimate sense of personal worth comes with something called "success."

This is why basic concerns for acceptance, competence, and control are so common in our society. When worth becomes a matter of achievement rather than being intrinsic to our nature as creatures of God, we must produce to be accepted. We must be competent to be respected. We'd better be in control, or we'll be controlled by someone else. These values emphasize independence and self-centeredness, rather than community and sharing.

Worst of all, as Kardiner says, "Success is a goal without a satiation point, and the desire for it, instead of abating, increases with achievement."[5]

That is a blueprint for anxiety. We were not made for that kind of life. Our self-concept needs to be formed in the context of God's love for us. Our relationships need to be such that we share life with each other in love and mutual respect.

The Spiritual Resources of the Community of Faith

Are the values of the community of faith different from the competitive individualism of modern western culture?

The psalms are very personal expressions and do not always reflect that David was a member of a close-knit community. The laws of the Old Testament were oriented toward the maintenance of Israel as a distinct community. The Israelites were supposed to treat each other specially, to care for and protect each other. This same orientation carried through in the New Testament community of believers.

The letter Paul wrote to the Christians at Ephesus is a fascinating example of the community of faith's values. Compare these values with competitive individualism.

First, the community of faith addresses our sense of self-worth by maintaining that worth is not built on success, or personal achievement, but on our nature as creatures of God. He made us, and he loves us. He valued us enough to die for us in Christ.

Paul said, "Praise be to the God and Father of our Lord Jesus Christ, who has blessed us in the heavenly realms with every spiritual blessing in Christ. For he chose us in him before the creation of the world to be holy and blameless in his sight. In love he predestined us to be adopted as his sons through Jesus Christ" (Eph. 1:3–5).

Second, the community of faith addresses our need for a network of nurturing relationships by emphasizing that we are members of each other. We belong to each other. We are citizens of a common heritage in Christ (2:13, 19).

Third, the community of faith provides for our specific needs for encouragement. When we face anxiety we need friends who will accept us with our anxiety. We need support that will not waver, and comfort that will not take advantage of our weakness.

Paul emphasized several important values that govern our interaction within the community of faith. Here relationships are marked by humility and gentleness. He exhorts us to be patient, bearing with one another in love (4:2).

We each have occupations, but these are not for our own personal aggrandizement. Instead we should use them to build each other up. The goal is to maintain unity, and to bring each other to full maturity so that our lives mirror Christ (4:14–16).

We are to be honest with each other, but not angry (4:25–26). We are not to use unwholesome talk that tears down, but are to try to build each other up according to our needs (4:29). We are not to hold grudges, but are to be forgiving (4:31–32). We are to encourage each other and enlarge our perspectives by sharing in worship (5:19).

In the community of faith, a new kind of love governs our relationships with each other. This love is a reflection of the love God has for us. Miriama Ba made a beautiful expression of the kind of relationship there should be between a husband and wife. I think it expresses the way people in the community of faith can and do relate to each other.

> To love one another! If only each partner could move sincerely towards each other! If each could only melt into the other! If each would only accept the other's qualities instead of listing his faults! If each could only correct bad habits without harping on about them! If each could penetrate the other's most secret haunts to forestall failure and be a support while tending to the evils that are repressed![6]

Best of all, in the community of faith we find people who say, "Even if your worst fears come true, we will not abandon you. We will stay with you and care for you and comfort you."

In this way, the community of faith becomes the living, flesh-and-blood expression of God's presence in our lives.

Some Tips for Helping in the Community of Faith

What has just been outlined is the ideal. Each of us has the responsibility to put it into practice. Here are some practical tips to keep in mind as we share comfort and strength with each other.

• *Be alert to the hints friends drop about anxieties.* We seldom share our anxieties without first testing the waters. Our culture teaches us to be wary of sharing anything that might be used against us. Instead, we offer each other furtive cries for help. Be sensitive to these and respond with an open heart.

• *Do not respond to anxiety with surprise.* All of us have some anxiety. Statistics show most of us will have at least one bout with severe anxiety during our lives. Instead of reacting with shock or surprise, accept anxiety as a normal occurrence that is significant, but manageable.

• *Don't downplay anxiety.* Our normal tendency is to try to talk people out of their anxiety with phrases like, "Oh, that's just an irrational thought! You're such a strong person. You don't need to be afraid." If a friend's anxiety is strong enough to be talked about, it needs to be taken seriously. The thoughts and feelings are real, regardless of their rationality. We need to accept them before we can be of help.

• *Don't rebuke.* The last thing we need when facing

anxiety is to be told, "shape up," or "get your act together," or "you know better than this."

• *Offer calm support and assurance.* Our friends need to know we understand and support them no matter what they feel like or what happens to them. Even if we don't understand everything going through their minds, we must give them our support. The sufferer needs to be reassured we will stand with them, and that things will eventually turn out all right.

• *Look for ways to help clarify what the fear is about.* Try to help those suffering to enlarge their vision, to see the positive aspects they may be ignoring. As they can pinpoint their fear, see if you can help them develop more realistic perspectives on the issue that has triggered their fear alarm.

• *Finally, pray.* In your prayer, emphasize praise and worship. Try to focus the attention of the one who suffers anxiety on the grace, strength, and constant presence of God. Ask God to intervene on behalf of the one who suffers, both to resolve the issue that has caused anxiety, and to give the person a real inner sense of his presence.

Lessons on the Importance of the Community of Faith

I will always be grateful for the experiences God gave me in Haiti. They were strenuous. They took me to my limits and beyond. But I learned so much.

My Haitian brothers and sisters taught me no lesson more powerfully than the one I've been discussing in this chapter—the importance of the community of faith for helping each other through life's difficult circumstances.

They taught me in many ways.

Haiti is a land where many people go without adequate food. In my years among them I never heard a Haitian Christian pray before a meal without asking God to provide for those who were less fortunate.

They were quick to confront a brother or sister who

had fallen into sin, but their discipline was never aimed at ostracizing or breaking fellowship.

Jerry and Lisa were short-term missionaries whose support got hung up in bureaucratic tangles for a while. When their supplies ran out they had no money to buy more. Deeply moved, Jerry told me of the knock that came at their front door one day. A Haitian brother stood there with food for them. Gifts of precious food, collected from sparse resources, continued until Jerry's support came through.

One of my greatest privileges was visiting village churches set far back in the mountains of southern Haiti. The mountains have their own barren beauty, folded ridge on ridge. Streams and rivers cut down through the valleys. Scrub bushes dot the mountainsides like thin stubble.

My visit to Elim was unforgettable. Our two-ton truck took us over the mountains on a one-lane road to Bainet, a provincial town on the south coast.

Bainet sits on a blue lagoon ringed by mountains. A river empties itself into the lagoon, spreading its brown stain into the sea during the rainy season. Women do their laundry where the river and the sea meet, looking like resting gulls when you first come round the curve. The market is always bustling. It is the only place to buy provisions in that area.

After our four-hour truck ride, we rested in a pastor's home. Basins of cool water were brought with soap and fresh towels so we could wash the dust of the road from our faces and necks. That done, we enjoyed conversation until our meal of rice, goat stew, tomatoes, and avocadoes was prepared.

When it came time to start our journey once again, mules and horses were loaded. We mounted and set out on the best part of the trip. For four-and-a-half hours we rode alongside and through the river, back up into the mountains. The path was busy with travelers going up and down, some heading home into the mountains, others going to Bainet on business.

My two missionary companions and I were always objects of great interest, and often of laughter. At one point one mule decided to rest and promptly sat down. My friend jerked frantically on the reins, uttering various imprecations in English. The mule didn't understand.

Nearby, two young Haitian girls all but collapsed on the ground in laughter at the spectacle of this strange American awkwardly straddling the mule who was by now resting comfortably on the ground.

Eventually we arrived at our destination, the Elim church. It is set on the top of a mountain from which ridges fan out in all directions. We were invited to make use of the little mud-walled, dirt-floored Sunday-school hut beside the rough stone church.

Again basins of water were brought for us. In a while the pastor's wife brought us a delicious meal of rice and goat meat. We washed up and ate before an audience of very curious children.

But the most unforgettable experiences of the trip were still to come. We had come to visit the local congregation and share with them in worship. That evening as we stood beside the church before the service, we watched the flickering lights of people making their way along the ridges to the church. Worship was lively and warm.

The next day was Sunday. Hundreds of people packed themselves into the church to share in worship. As I sat on the platform and looked out on the sea of faces waiting to hear what I had to say, I began to feel uncomfortable. What did I have to give them? How little I really understood of their lives, the hardships they faced, their unique joys. Yet here they were, waiting to hear me. I wanted them to teach me about their faith, which had been hammered out through years of patiently endured hardship.

They did teach me. At the close of the service, the pastor and I served communion. A gaily colored tray was brought with red and yellow plastic glasses. Juice was mixed and poured, hard Haitian bread broken on the tray.

We had been at worship for about four hours, but they were in no hurry to leave. This was the most important part of their week. With these elements we observed the ancient service of Holy Communion.

They knelt on the worn concrete floor, but not silently. As I passed before them their hands reached up to take the bread and juice. I was awestruck listening to their prayers, watching their faces, feeling their living faith.

Their lives were far more difficult than mine has ever been. Some prayed for sick loved ones. Others for forgiveness. Some prayed for the provision of their needs. All of them poured out their hearts to God, in concert, lifting each other, finding courage and comfort in the real presence of God in that old stone church on a Haitian mountain.

Together they were his children. They were a community of faith, belonging together, carrying each other through life.

This is one of our most blessed resources as children of God. We have his presence with us. We have his ceaseless grace. And we have the living, flesh-and-blood presence of our brothers and sisters. We have their voices to pray with us when our fears weigh us down. We have their smiles of encouragement. We have their hands to reach across the empty spaces, in the dark moments, to say with a squeeze, or a pat on the back, "I'm with you."

NOTES

[1]*Soeur* is the French word for sister.

[2]Robert Frost, "Revelation," *Robert Frost: Poems* (New York: Pocket Books, 1946, 1971), 155.

[3]Rollo May, *The Meaning of Anxiety* (New York: The Ronald Press, 1950), 152.

[4]Ibid., 158.

[5]Ibid., 163.

[6]Miriama Ba, *So Long A Letter* (London: Heinemann Educational Books Ltd., 1980), 88–89.

9
CREATING A CLIMATE OF CONFIDENCE

We've arrived at the final chapter in our study. We've discovered the nature of fear—that it's an alarm system given to us by God for our protection. We've seen why and how the system can go awry, why we need to talk about conquering fear. We've talked about the deep spiritual resources God gives us to do that.

There's a final bit of truth to consider before we end. We need to think about maintaining a general inner climate that helps us maintain a tone of confidence and peace. In order to keep on conquering fear, our lives need an inner climate of confidence.

Replacing Timidity

We've seen how David was able to meet life's threatening circumstances with courage—the habits of heart and mind he developed to help him. David found ways to create an inner climate of confidence for his life. This helped him face the challenges that called forth fear.

For many of us, the climate of our lives seems harried and upset. We're always on the edge of anxiety. We face life with quivering souls, waiting for the next blow, for the disaster we know is waiting around the corner. We trade the sure peace of today for the possible trouble of tomorrow. The inner climate of our lives is one of timidity instead of confidence.

Paul said something about this to Timothy. Apparently, Timothy struggled with this problem. Paul's letters often offered encouragement and confidence.

He wrote, "Don't let anyone look down on you because you are young, but set an example for the believers" (1 Tim. 4:12). On another occasion he gave these instructions to the people Timothy would visit in Corinth. "If Timothy comes, see to it that he has nothing to fear while he is with you" (1 Cor. 16:10).

At one point Paul wrote to Timothy, "For God did not give us a spiriit of timidity, but a spirit of power, of love and of self-discipline" (2 Tim. 1:7).

The word Paul used for timidity has the sense of cowardice. Remember cowardice? Cowardice is the spirit that quails before challenges, that refuses to take them on with the resources available.

In place of timidity, or cowardice, Paul reminded Timothy that God has given us three traits—power, love, and self-discipline. Once again, the words he used are significant. They are *dunamis, agape,* and *sophronismos.*

Dunamis is the inexhaustible energy that comes from God. The huge engines that drive ocean-going ships used to be called *dynamos,* a word related to the word *dunamis.* Those engines could pound away hour after hour, day after day, month after month, churning out the power to drive the ship through night and day, calm and storm. In the same way, God's power is available to us to replace timidity. God's power isn't weakened by the elements or by the circumstances of our lives. It remains the same all the time, equal to all our tests.

Agape is the giving love, the love that shifts our vision from ourselves to others. It is made possible when God is enshrined in our hearts.

Sophronismos is an interesting trait. It means self-discipline that draws upon moderation, good judgment, and prudence. These qualities are extremely important in replacing the climate of timidity with the climate of confidence.

Fear drives us to extremes of feeling and action. Moderation makes us take a step back for a moment. What is true about these feelings? What is useful about our contemplated actions?

Good judgment forces fear to account for itself. What does it have to teach us? How can we best tackle it?

Prudence guides our choices, making us reject those that would bring us into unnecessary danger, or fill our minds unnecessarily with unwholesome, frightening, or degrading images.

The point is this: God has given us spiritual resources and has made possible character traits that can replace our timidity with a climate of confidence. Rather than facing life with a continual attitude of timidity and cowardice, we need to develop and maintain a spirit of confidence. As we put into practice the habits outlined here and draw on our spiritual resources, this can become a reality for us. Little by little we can retrain our minds and hearts, and God can put into us an inner climate of confidence.

This may take time. It will also take practice. We won't change life-long habits of timidity with confidence overnight. If we've spent years weaning our minds on images of disaster and thoughts of doom, those habits won't go away without work.

Remember this: Our fears may come uninvited, but we have a choice of what to do with them when they come. Thoughts can come into the mind that seem entirely out of our control. We may face a threatening circumstance and automatically begin to believe we're defeated. Those recurring thoughts and images may push us to the brink of panic almost before we can react. But God has given us control of our mind. That means we can choose how to react to circumstances, and to thoughts.

Here are some practical steps we can take to help replace our inner climate of timidity with a climate of confidence.

Analysis

The first priority is to develop the habit of analysis. Those who struggle most with timidity have a habit of allowing emotions to dominate their responses to life's events and circumstances.

For example, if the rumor mill at work churns out the hot tip that cutbacks are coming, and that their jobs will be the next to go, their emotions take over. Immediately their stomachs squeeze into little knots. They start wondering how they'll survive, who'll make the house payment, what they'll do next. Their emotions have taken over and they've surrendered their power of choice.

Or if someone says something unusual, or does something that appears unkind or unjust, they start wondering. Now why did he do that? What have I done? Does he still like me? This whole tumbling line of thought can quickly slide into lowered self-esteem, and into the agony of fear. Emotions have taken over.

We need to learn how to slow down the process, how to think rationally about events and circumstances. We need to develop the ability to analyze the events and our feelings about them.

In analyzing fear we should ask the following questions.

1. Do my emotions have physical sources, or are they exacerbated by illness or exhaustion? Could there be physiological disturbances involved?

If the answer to these questions is yes, then we seek the help of qualified medical professionals. If we've been ill or have exhausted our physical resources of strength and immunity, our emotional balance will be unsteady. If our acute anxiety has come on suddenly, and we cannot find any good reason for it, we should not hesitate to ask for our doctor's advice. A physician will be able to help us decide whether physiological causes are involved, and where to go from there.

2. Do my emotions reflect major issues in my life that need to be resolved? Are there recurring mental images or automatic thoughts that need to be modified?

It may take time and some reflection to answer these questions. But if the answer seems to be yes, if there seem to be issues that repeatedly trouble us, or if we are plagued by recurring images and thoughts that bring us to the brink of panic or which we find extremely unpleasant, we have a couple of courses open. First, we can seek qualified counselors who can help us resolve those issues and modify those recurring images and thoughts. Second, we can practice the kind of homework made possible by books like this one. Both are valid courses of action.

3. Have traumatic or unsettling events taken place in my life that might be linked to my emotions?

We need to be aware that research shows us to be especially susceptible to fear when our lives are upset. If we've recently gone through major upheavals like a move, a divorce, a bereavement, a change in jobs, or major surgery, we'll be more susceptible to fear. If we face some continuing source of extreme tension or pressure, our emotions will be affected and we'll be more susceptible to fear. Continuing financial pressure, or work demands are examples of this kind of tension.

We develop a climate of confidence by making it a habit to face fear with analysis instead of raw emotion. Undoubtedly, we will feel certain emotions under certain circumstances, but we reserve the power of choice as to what we will do about those feelings and circumstances.

This process allows us to begin putting into practice the steps outlined in this book, and to begin drawing on our spiritual resources.

Practical Tools for Breaking Fear's Grasp

Here are some practical tools we can use to help maintain our confidence and equilibrium when we're in the grasp of fear.

Activity. Fear often freezes us into inactivity. Fear tends to make us think we can't do anything but sit and wait for our doom.

Counselors suggest that this is something of a self-feeding mechanism. The more we give in to this feeling, the more acute our fear becomes, and the less able we are to break free of its grasp. Initiating some activity, no matter how mundane, often has the power to break fear's monopoly.

One way to break fear's grasp is to engage in some activity that can distract our minds from the fear. Constructive activity that absorbs our attention and gives us a sense of achievement is a good way of breaking fear's hold on our minds long enough for us to begin to think clearly.

Relaxation. Fear also has the power to seize control of our physical processes. Acute anxiety and panic are characterized by several unpleasant physical sensations. Our breathing becomes rapid and uneven. We may feel a great sense of physical discomfort without being able to pinpoint what that sensation is. We may become dizzy and disoriented. Numbness of hands and arms is not unusual. Along with these, we lose our ability to think clearly. Our minds may become fuzzy.

There are several useful techniques to combat these physical sensations. In fact, the first step a counselor will take to treat acute anxiety and panic is to help get physical symptoms under control.

These physical symptoms can be controlled. There are many techniques to help us do so. To learn more about them a useful resource is *The Relaxation & Stress Reduction Workbook, 2nd Edition.*[1]

One popular and useful technique has to do with breathing relaxation. The rapid, shallow breathing connected with fear contributes to hyperventilation, which in turn heightens anxiety. The breathing relaxation technique begins by focusing your thinking on your breathing. Draw your breath in slowly and deeply through your nose, hold it for a moment, and then let it out slowly through your mouth. As you do this, think only of your breath. Don't allow your attention to be claimed by the clamoring images and thoughts that rush through your mind. If they come, just say to yourself, "I'll think about that later. Right now I need to think about my breathing." Continue to do this until you begin to feel yourself relaxing.

I've used this breathing relaxation technique to good advantage. It's simple but effective. It won't make whatever triggered your fear go away, but it will help you get control of the physical symptoms of your fear. From there you can go on to further steps.

Another simple technique often used in therapists' offices has to do with imaging. We've pointed out in earlier chapters that a large part of fear's power is in its ability to monopolize our mental imagery. When we are gripped by fear, our mental imagery is catastrophic—we believe something terrible is happening or about to happen to us. Our mental imagery is limited. We can only see the disaster, and none of the extenuating and helpful forces that may be ours.

Imaging is sometimes used in New Age settings, but the therapeutic technique known by that name should not be identified exclusively with that movement, since it grows out of sound psychological insights. Those insights are available to Christians. Used correctly, imaging can be a powerful tool to help break fear's monopoly over our emotions.

To use this technique you are told by the therapist to get into a comfortable position. You may be asked to bring along some music you like, music that puts you in a good mood. Then you are asked to imagine yourself in some setting you find very pleasant. It may be a white sandy beach, under a graceful palm tree beneath sun-sparkling blue skies, beside a crystal lagoon. You imagine the sound of the slight breeze as it tickles the sand and rustles the long, slender palm leaves. It is peaceful and quiet. In your hand is a cold tropical fruit punch. You have no pressures. Your problems are gone. You just lie there and relax, drinking in the beauty and peace.

That scene may not be your particular image of pleasure, but the point is to try to immerse yourself in some image that replaces your fearful imagery. As you keep this up for several minutes, you will find yourself relaxing, and the fear receding. Try this sometime when your mind is inundated with fear that won't leave you alone.

This is not a substitute for dealing with the underlying issues that triggered the fear, but it is a way to break the immediate grasp of fear so that you can take further steps.

Balance. Another way we lessen the power of fear is by maintaining balance in our lives. We need to balance the mental and physical input and output of our lives.

By taking care with our diet, making time for mental and emotional relaxation, and engaging in regular exercise we help ward off some of the forces that exacerbate anxiety. Driving ourselves to exhaustion without providing time to rest and replenish our mental and physical strength is asking for trouble.

Each of us must find our own level on this point. For example, I've found that when my supplies of energy get depleted, simply working hard is usually not the problem. Instead, I've found that the mental and emotional intensity demanded by the task is more important than the physical exertion required. One way body and mind let me know when I've reached the limit is that my emotions get out of trim. That's when I need to pay attention to the balance of my life.

We must also pay attention to the balance of what we feed our minds. It would be foolish to feed ourselves on a steady mental diet of negative or frightening material, and then be surprised when the climate of our lives is one of timidity instead of confidence. This does not mean we face life with unrealistic rosy glasses; it means we recognize that if we spend our conversations talking about the terrible events that have happened, and that might happen in the future, we will set a particular emotional tone for our lives. If we take in a steady diet of degrading and horrible "entertainment," we can expect that to set a particular emotional tone. In neither of these cases will that tone be one that helps us face life with an inner climate of confidence.

Maintaining Confidence

Confidence has images of communion and cooperation at its center. It implies being and working with someone else. It implies the opposite of isolation and loneliness.

Think of the word itself. It comes from the root of the Latin word *fidere.* That word means "to trust." The prefix "con," means *"with.* Thus, confidence is a matter of trusting with, or of having faith with someone or something else.

What a wonderful concept for those choosing to walk with God! Confidence comes as we are united with him. It is built on a together trust. Confidence is having faith together with God—faith in his grace and power, faith in our shared relationship.

God gives himself to us in total commitment. We give ourselves to him in faith, in complete surrender. Out of this oneness comes the possibility of a re-creation of the inner climate of our lives.

Here is the possibility for true dignity, joy, sturdiness—for an inner climate of confidence. This was where David got his inner climate of confidence. It's where all who walk in close fellowship with God find the strength to face life with joy and peace.

Jeremiah is another Bible character who learned this secret of confidence. There wasn't much in Jeremiah's life to make it peaceful. And yet, listen to his words. I can't help but believe he had learned this lesson well.

"Cursed is the one who trusts in man,
  who depends on flesh for his strength
  and whose heart turns away from the LORD.
He will be like a bush in the wastelands;
  he will not see prosperity when it comes.
He will dwell in the parched places of the desert,

in a salt land where no one lives.

But blessed is the man who trusts in the LORD,
    whose confidence is in him.
He will be like a tree planted by the water
    that sends out its roots by the stream.
It does not fear when heat comes;
    its leaves are always green.
It has no worries in a year of drought
    and never fails to bear fruit."
(Jer. 17:5–8)

We gain and maintain an inner climate of confidence by entering into the kind of relationship with God depicted in these lines. It was the confidence of David. It was the strength of Paul. It can also be our strength.

I'd like to share a final illustration from my life in Haiti. Off the west coast of Haiti is a small island called La Gonave. La Gonave is about forty-five miles long and fifteen miles wide. There isn't much there except for hills, scrub trees, and villages dotted here and there. About fifty thousand people live on the island.

The mission I worked for operated the only hospital on that island, with the only resident doctors and nurses. Almost all of the movement from La Gonave to the main island is by small, open, Haitian sailboats.

Those boats are marvels. There isn't a straight board in them. The planks are rough, hand-hewn boards. The chinks between them are filled with pith and tar. The single mast is usually made of the tallest tree available. I never saw one with a straight mast. The sails are usually old, tattered canvas. But the boats have plied the waters around the islands for hundreds of years and will probably go on doing so for a long time.

A recent innovation has been to add outboard motors to these boats. Our mission boat usually carried a sail and two small motors. I often wondered why it was necessary to fly a sail while running motors. When I once asked the captain about it, he just shrugged and told me it was better that way. It was a lesson I was to learn vividly.

I made the two-hour passage across the fourteen-mile stretch of sea between La Gonave and the main island many times. That channel, while often calm, can also be churned by strong winds into high waves. I remember well one passage we made. About a dozen of us were on board, including my wife and two little daughters. Luggage and freight were piled high in the open center of the boat. We sat on hard benches around the sides. The Haitian captain and his mate put up the sail, started one of the motors, and we set out.

Not long afterwards the wind began to blow. Soon we were pitching up and down the sides of six to nine foot waves. It was cold. The wind whipped the water across the open boat until we were all drenched. But the little boat pushed steadily through the water, driven by the sail and the motor.

Suddenly, with a crack louder than a gunshot the sail tore to shreds from one side to the other. The little boat began to gyrate even more. The mate got the shredded sail down quickly. Now the lone motor was all that pushed us along.

Just as I was thanking God for that motor, it began to sputter, then quit. We were drifting between waves that looked twice as large as they had a moment before. I knew the danger of getting sideways to the waves and of being rolled over. We were helpless.

Quickly the captain tried to restart the motor. When it refused, he bent over the back-up motor. We held our breath as he switched the fuel line and jerked the starter cord. Would it start?

To our great relief, after a couple of pulls, the little

engine barked to life and began purring away. Once again we were under way. During the rest of the trip we thanked God for his protection, and for a motor that kept us on course. What seemed an eternity later, we came alongside our dock. We were cold, wet to the skin, and never wanted to ride in that boat again.

From that experience I learned the use of a sail. Even when you have a motor to drive the boat, the pressure of the wind on the sail holds the boat steady. It keeps it from bobbing and gyrating in the waves. The motor will drive it, but the sail drives it and keeps it steady.

The steadiness the sail gives the little boat illustrates what I mean by the steadiness we receive from an inner climate of confidence.

As we enjoy a living, working relationship with God, and as we make use of the powerful resources he makes available, we are given the confidence to face all that life holds, with peace. That inner climate of confidence holds us steady.

Certainly life has events and circumstances that will be threatening. There is plenty of room in this world for fear. And yet, with these resources, we have what we need to conquer fear.

And so I leave you with a prayer that you may learn to pass through this life with peace, replacing timidity with confidence. It is a wonderful world, despite its frightening moments. It's a world to be enjoyed. We have a life worth living to its fullest.

May the LORD answer you when you are in
    distress;
  may the name of the God of Jacob protect you.
May he send you help from the sanctuary
  and grant you support from Zion.
May he remember all your sacrifices

and accept your . . . offerings.

May he give you the desire of your heart
   and make all your plans succeed.
We will shout for joy when you are victorious
   and will lift up our banners in the name of our
      God.
May the LORD grant all your requests.

Now I know that the LORD saves his anointed;
   he answers him from his holy heaven
   with the saving power of his right hand.
Some trust in chariots and some in horses,
   but we trust in the name of the LORD our God.
They are brought to their knees and fall,
   but we rise up and stand firm.

O LORD, . . .
   Answer us when we call!

(Psalm 20)

NOTES

[1]Martha Davis, Elizabeth Robbins Eshelman, Matthew McKay, *The Relaxation & Stress Reduction Workbook, 2nd Edition* (Oakland, CA: New Harbinger Publications, 1982).

CHAPTER
STUDY
GUIDES

1

THE DAILY ADVENTURE
OF LIVING
WITH CONFIDENCE

CHAPTER SUMMARY

Fear is a normal part of the human experience, even among Christians.

Fear disrupts life, drains spiritual strength, clouds judgment, and makes decisions difficult. Learning to conquer fear is one of the most important issues facing contemporary Christians.

The question at the heart of this book is: What unique spiritual resources do Christians have to face and conquer fear?

In order to do this, we will
1. define fear
2. outline a simple plan to use in facing fear
3. discover unique spiritual resources in the psalms for coping with fear

KEY IDEAS IN THIS CHAPTER

1. Fear is a part of everyone's life, even Christians' lives.
2. We cannot conquer fear until we begin to understand it.
3. The study of fear is a positive adventure, because it shows us ourselves.
4. Discovering God's provisions for conquering fear makes each day an adventure in confident living.

MASTER THIS: The great blessing of fear is that it shows us ourselves as we really are and forces us to dig deeply into our faith in Christ. The power of a living relationship with God does not exempt us from fear but gives us courage to conquer fear.

STUDY QUESTIONS

1. Reflect back over your life. Identify an experience that produced fear in you.
2. List five possible effects of fear upon us. Which of these did you feel as you passed through the fearful experience you identified above?
3. What three things will this book attempt to do?
4. In what ways can a study of fear be a positive adventure?
5. What resources do we have to enable us to conquer fear and live with confidence?

2

UNDERSTANDING OUR BUILT-IN ALARM

CHAPTER SUMMARY

Since fear produces strong physical, mental, and emotional responses, it has the power to focus our attention on our immediate feelings and limit our ability to think clearly.

It is necessary to understand fear in order to learn from it and move beyond it to peace and confidence. Therefore, we must learn to distinguish it from the following reactions:

1. Cowardice is withdrawing in the face of fear, giving in instead of going on.
2. Anger lashes out at the circumstances in self-defense, introducing destructive influences into the situation.

3. Worry mulls over a threat without arriving at the underlying cause or arriving at a solution.
4. Depression can have many causes and also magnifies fear.

Fear is a system of internal communication about events and circumstances of life, an alarm system triggered by anything physical, spiritual, or psychological that we interpret as a threat.

Anxiety is a less-defined form of fear, a longer-lasting, vague feeling of dread.

Fear does not fulfill its proper function in our lives when

1. we cannot or will not face the threat, blocking it out with alcohol, compulsive eating, overwork, or some other substitute for reality.
2. we misinterpret something harmless as a threat.

A proper understanding of the fears that plague us takes away their mystery and helps us to deal with them.

KEY IDEAS IN THIS CHAPTER

1. Cowardice, anger, worry, and depression are faulty ways of reacting to fear. We must move through and beyond these in order to deal with fear and to conquer it.
2. Fear is a system of internal communication that we develop about the events and circumstances of life.
3. That system malfunctions when we block it out or misinterpret a harmless incident as fearful.
4. We must face fear head-on and devise constructive ways to deal with it.

MASTER THIS: A proper understanding of fear is essential to keeping it in its right perspective. We can accept it as a God-given ability to detect and deal with danger. In God's mercy and love, he will give us the resources to live with normal fear and to conquer abnormal fear.

STUDY QUESTIONS

1. What does fear have the power to do?
2. What is the benefit of understanding fear?
3. List and define four things that are like fear but are not the same as fear.
4. Define fear.
5. Define anxiety.
6. How do fear and anxiety function as an alarm system?
7. In what two ways might this alarm system fail? Have you ever experienced one or both kinds of malfunction? Explain.
8. In what two ways does an understanding of fear help us?
9. How does God help us face our fears?
10. Restate the two concluding statements of this chapter.

3

TAKING THE
INTERACTIVE APPROACH

CHAPTER SUMMARY

No matter how terrible our experiences of fear, something in us seeks to survive.

There are at least three ways to approach the problem of fear.

1. We can face fear passively and become its victims.
2. We can take on fear actively and become its adversaries.
3. We can face fear interactively and become adventurers using fear constructively, challenging it, and forcing it to work for us.

It is necessary to find out what triggers our "fear alarm," to search out the underlying causes and clarify them. The following are helpful in doing this:

1. prayer and meditation on our circumstances
2. counsel of trusted friends
3. professional counselors if necessary

We must not limit ourselves by dealing with emotions that spring out of our fears. We must go to the source of our fears through the interactive approach. This means we work through causes of fear and eliminate them with planned strategies.

Things that trigger fear are often complex and require time and thought to understand. They are sometimes tied to psychological or physiological causes. These problems often require the help of a health professional.

KEY IDEAS IN THIS CHAPTER

1. We must search out the underlying causes of our fears in order to conquer them.
2. Using the interactive approach to conquering fear in our lives means that we take steps to eliminate the sources of fear, or modify disturbing thought patterns and mental images.
3. We must replace old ways of looking at life with new ways that address the sources of our unrest.

MASTER THIS: The interactive approach to dealing with fear releases God's resources in our walk with him, so that stability, courage, and hope conquer the power of fear in our lives.

STUDY QUESTIONS

1. List three ways to approach the problem of fear.
2. Define the "interactive approach."
3. What is the first step in the interactive approach to fear?
4. Point out the difference between the immediate trigger of our fear alarm and the underlying causes.

5. List three sources of help in identifying underlying causes of fear.
6. What is the second step in the interactive approach to fear?
7. Why is it difficult to pinpoint the causes of some fears?
8. List some physical or emotional causes of fear that may need the help of a health professional.
9. Go back to the personal experience you related in chapter one. Use your experience to develop the steps in the interactive approach. Do you still need to apply these steps to your fear?

4

RAISING COURAGE
IN THE SANCTUARY
OF GOD'S PRESENCE

CHAPTER SUMMARY

In order to cope with fear we need five things: courage, stability, perspective, comfort, and hope.

Fearful experiences test our mettle, or courage, as illustrated by the author's experience in Haiti. Courage helps us to think more clearly in the face of danger and to pinpoint the issues at stake, coming to a wise course of action.

We must choose to go to the sanctuary of God's presence to raise courage. Psalm 11 illustrates how David made the sanctuary of God's presence his habitual way of responding to threats.

1. David identified the threat.
2. He weighed options before him.

3. He took practical steps to deal with the threat.

The sanctuary of God is a place set apart, a holy place where only those persons and things that conform to God's nature can dwell. Psalm 15 indicates that if we want access to the sanctuary of God's presence, we must live in right relationship with God and in charity and harmony with fellow human beings.

The sanctuary of God's presence gives new reserves of courage to face daily life with joy just as it comes to us (Psalm 16).

KEY IDEAS IN THIS CHAPTER

1. Courage is mental or moral strength to venture, persevere, and withstand danger, fear, or difficulty. It is an ingrained capacity for meeting strain or difficulty with fortitude and resilience.
2. Courage gives us the ability to put fear on hold while we examine its causes and decide on a course of action to deal with it.
3. Courage is developed in the sanctuary of God's presence.
4. A sanctuary is a place set apart, a holy place. If we want access to this sanctuary, we must live in a right relationship with God and in charity and harmony with fellow human beings.
5. Anxiety is conquered as we habitually enter the sanctuary of God for nurture and guidance.

MASTER THIS: When anxiety comes, we can make it a habit to suspend those first panic-stricken thoughts and turn to the holy sanctuary of God's presence. It is there that we receive courage to cope with anxiety and where the living presence of God sets us free from fear.

STUDY QUESTIONS

1. What do we need to develop to conquer fear?
2. What is the spiritual resource for courage?
3. What fantasy do we sometimes create about fear?
4. Define *courage*.
5. Complete this statement: Courage puts anxiety on hold and says, _____.
6. How do we develop courage?
7. List the three steps David followed in Psalm 11 to deal with fear.
8. Memorize Psalm 9:9–10 and 20:7. Write these verses below and repeat them.
9. Define the word *sanctuary*, giving the meaning of the root word.
10. From Psalm 15, describe the kind of person who feels comfortable in the holy sanctuary of God's presence.
11. List some of the substitutes people rely on for courage instead of the sanctuary of God's presence.
12. Have you found the joy described in Psalm 16 in the midst of life's difficult circumstances? If not, what do you need to do to make the sanctuary of God your habitual refuge?

5
BUILDING A
STABLE LIFE FOUNDATION

CHAPTER SUMMARY

Anxiety (fear) is characterized by a sense of vulnerability.

We cannot always escape from circumstances that cause vulnerability, as illustrated by the story about Ron. In order to cope, it is necessary to find a way to face this sense of vulnerability that lies behind our anxiety. Instead of escape, we need a solid foundation from which to face and resolve anxiety—the solid foundation of a living relationship with God.

In this life two crucial exchanges take place:

1. Grace for guilt. Guilt that comes from sin produces fear, an aching unsettled feeling inside, an inner sense of vulnerability because of moral failure, and

also produces feelings against others (Psalm 38).
God's answer to guilt is absolution through grace,
an infinite reservoir of forgiveness for those who
confess, not abolition of moral standards. Grace is
the answer to the fear that springs from moral
failure.
2. Reverence for pride. To be in God's presence
commands either panic born of guilt, or reverence
born of worship (reverential fear). Reverential fear
becomes a part of our lives when we surrender
willful pride, making him Lord of our lives. Reverential fear makes it possible to face ourselves
honestly, to face our own vulnerabilities.

These exchanges make possible a daily conversation
with God, which in turn gives us confidence instead of
timidity in spite of the vulnerabilities of life (Psalm 127).

KEY IDEAS IN THIS CHAPTER
1. Anxiety is characterized by vulnerability.
2. We cannot always escape the circumstances that
cause vulnerability, so we need a solid foundation
from which to face life and cope with our vulnerabilities.
3. Living with Christ is a shared experience between
two committed persons, Christ and me. It is
essential to building a stable foundation.
4. Two crucial exchanges take place in this life in
Christ—grace for guilt, and reverence for pride.
5. This makes daily conversation with God possible,
which in turn gives confidence instead of timidity
as we face the events of this life—a stable life
foundation.

MASTER THIS: Living in Christ means an ongoing relationship with a living, caring Being who keeps us in his

thoughts and love. It is a shared "conversation" between two committed individuals—God and me, providing freedom from guilt and giving me the proper reverence toward him who is able to direct my life and deliver me from fear.

STUDY QUESTIONS

1. Anxiety is always characterized by a sense of ＿＿＿
＿＿＿＿＿＿＿＿＿＿＿＿＿＿＿＿＿＿＿.
2. Explain what it means to be vulnerable.
3. What secure foundation does a Christian have for facing the twists and turns of life?
4. Define "conversation" as it refers to the Christian life.
5. Explain the exchange of "grace for guilt."
6. What causes guilty fear?
7. By what standard do we establish moral values?
8. What is David's greatest anxiety in Psalm 38?
9. Do you need to deal with guilt in your own life? What can you do about it?
10. Explain the exchange of "reverence for pride."
11. What stands in the way of reverential fear of God?
12. Do you have a daily conversation with God? If not, what do you need to do to have this stable life foundation?

6
GAINING PERSPECTIVE
THROUGH PRAISE

CHAPTER SUMMARY

To conquer fear, we need enlarged perspectives. Praise enables us to modify catastrophic mental images and overcome tunnel vision that feeds fear.

Anxiety attacks are real and come from recurring mental images and automatic thoughts usually imbedded in some event in the past. Usually they

1. are images of catastrophe
2. assume the feeling of reality
3. narrow our mental vision and limit its scope

In order to deal with fear resulting from these images, we must take two steps:

1. Pinpoint the mental imagery that leads to anxiety and begin to consciously modify that imagery.

2. Dig deeper to discover the source of these mental images.

We can consciously modify the fearful imagery of our minds by setting up a grid of questions from Philippians 4:8–9. Are the mental images noble, right, pure, lovely, admirable? We then strive to change the ones that deviate from those qualities. We do this through worship and praise.

David is our example in Psalm 3. His formula is to

1. pinpoint the threat
2. enter the sanctuary of God's presence
3. ask God to intervene
4. fix the mind on specific images of victory and peace

The key to modifying fearful imagery is worship of God—concentrating on his nature, which issues in praise as in Psalm 16.

We do not praise events or circumstances—we may be thankful for them. We praise God for who he is in spite of events or circumstances.

Praise is a powerful resource in helping us to change images, because it focuses on the nature of God, full of grace and love (Rom. 8:35, 39).

KEY THOUGHTS

1. Catastrophic mental images feed fear and must be replaced with realistic thoughts.
2. Psalm 3 gives the formula for modifying these mental images:
    a. Pinpoint the source.
    b. Run to God (worship).
    c. Ask God to intervene.
    d. Praise God by fixing the mind on images of victory and praise.

3. Praising God modifies catastrophic mental images and overcomes tunnel vision that feeds fear.

4. We gain another perspective through praise because it focuses our minds on the loving and gracious nature of God.

MASTER THIS: We can change fearful mental imagery by praising God for who he is, filling our minds with his goodness and love, even though we may not thank him for difficult circumstances.

STUDY QUESTIONS

1. What is "catastrophic" mental imagery?
2. What triggers this thought process?
3. Give three characteristics of catastrophic mental images.
4. What are the two steps we need to take in order to deal with catastrophic mental images?
5. How can we deal with the fearful imagery of being spiritually lost?
6. Using Philippians 4:8, what kinds of questions can we use to modify mental imagery?
7. Give four steps in Psalm 3 for overcoming fearful thoughts.
8. The key to becoming victorious over fear is _____ _____, which results in praise.
9. What is the object of praise?
10. Describe how praise is a powerful resource for overcoming fear.
11. What fearful imagery does your mind produce at times? (This could be about a possible accident, loss of a loved one, loss of financial security, becoming terminally ill, being spiritually lost.)
12. What steps will you take to begin the habit of worship and praise in order to change these thoughts?

7

FINDING HOPE
IN PERSONAL HISTORY

CHAPTER SUMMARY

Anxiety seldom leads to violence, but the story of Okonkwo illustrates two important facts about anxiety:
1. It can be traced to origins in our personal history.
2. We are doomed to wrestle with anxiety until we deal with it redemptively.

We face life out of our "cognitive set," or the mental context created by our personal history. It guides the way we interpret and respond to life events.

Conquering anxiety requires clarifying and dealing with basic concerns and assumptions by exploring our personal history. This means facing it squarely and using it redemptively.

As we examine our past we can see the footsteps of

God moving through our history with us. In the psalms we see David's bottomless well of living hope within his "cognitive set." In Psalms 4 and 25, we have the formula for overcoming fear with hope:

1. Turn to the sanctuary of God for refuge.
2. Affirm God's presence in our history.
3. Affirm hope for the future instead of despair.

Our cognitive set is made up of four kinds of data: feelings, thoughts, assumptions, and issues. Out of these spring the mind's interpretation of present experiences.

We have the power to choose to change these habits of thought by carefully examining our personal history and finding good in those experiences the mind perceives as fearful and dangerous.

The hope we have as we trace the footprints of God through our past and into our present is one of the most precious spiritual resources we have for conquering fear.

KEY THOUGHTS

1. We face life out of our "cognitive set," or mental context created by our personal history. It guides the way we interpret and respond to life events.
2. Usually our recurring anxieties revolve around one or two central issues coming out of our cognitive set.
3. Clearly facing our basic concerns gives us a chance to work with anxiety objectively, to challenge our assumptions, and to free ourselves to develop more realistic and positive approaches to life.
4. Conquering anxiety requires clarifying and dealing with our personal history, tracing God's footprints there, and using the information gained redemptively. This means seeing good in bad experiences.
5. The hope which springs out of tracing the foot-

prints of God through our past and into our present is one of the most precious spiritual resources we have for conquering fear.

MASTER THIS: We can conquer fear as we face our own personal history, understand our "cognitive set," and trace the footprints of God through our past. Hope springs to life as we choose to see the difficult events of our past redemptively.

STUDY QUESTIONS

1. Name the facts about anxiety that are learned from the story of Okonkwo.
2. Define "cognitive set."
3. Give two examples of how our anxieties usually revolve around one or two central issues coming out of our cognitive set.
4. In order to deal with our basic concerns, we need to _____

   _____

   _____

   _____

5. What is the spiritual resource we have for dealing with our personal history?
6. In Psalms 4 and 25, David uses three steps in dealing with anxiety. What are they?

   _____

   _____

   _____

   _____

   _____

   _____

7. Trace the grace of God (his footsteps) in one fearful event in your personal history.

8. List four kinds of data that make up our cognitive set.
9. We are almost always aware of one of these before all the others. Which one?
10. Describe the process by which we explore our personal history in order to arrive at an understanding of the basic issues that disturb us.
11. From the author's experience of exploring his personal history for causes of anxiety, show how he dealt with it redemptively in order to change his habitual thought pattern.
12. Do you recognize an anxiety thought pattern that comes out of your cognitive set? State it, and then list the evidence of God's footsteps in your personal history that can help you to change your thought patterns.

8

FINDING COMFORT
IN THE COMMUNITY
OF FAITH

CHAPTER SUMMARY

To conquer fear, we need the solace of nurturing relationships. The community of faith provides a network of relationships marked by trust, acceptance, and reassurance. The story of Soeur Marie illustrates the concept that everyone is important in this community of faith. There are no "extras."

A review of chapters 4–7 shows the spiritual resources we need to overcome anxiety:

1. A place of sanctuary to retreat to
2. A stable life foundation
3. An attitude of worship and praise
4. Hope, from dealing redemptively with our personal history

The fifth spiritual resource needed to overcome anxiety is nurturing relationships in the body of Christ. This helps us by

1. providing a healthy way to open up about our self-image
2. providing shared respect, mutual trust, and active love

The competitive individualism of our culture makes three issues common causes of anxiety:

1. the need for acceptance
2. the need for competence
3. the need for control

The pressure of "living up to your potential" has placed emphasis on individual achievement rather than community. This affects our sense of self-worth, and when this goes awry, it impacts our personal relationships.

The community of faith places value on people rather than achievement. The emphasis on persons in the psalms carries over into the New Testament. Ephesians addresses these concepts in the following ways:

1. Our worth is based on the fact that God made us and he loves us (1:3–5).
2. We are members of one another, part of a nurturing fellowship (2:13–22).
3. The community of faith provides our specific need for encouragement (5:19).

Seven tips are given to us for helping someone else in the community of faith.
They are:

1. _____.
2. _____.
3. _____.

4. _____.
5. _____.
6. _____.
7. _____.

KEY THOUGHTS

1. To conquer fear we need the solace of nurturing relationships.
2. Some of our greatest spiritual resources for conquering life's threatening circumstances are to be found in the community of faith.
3. Because of the underlying cultural value of competitive individualism, we are constantly pressured to "live up to our potential." Our value system places great importance on achievement rather than on people.
4. The community of faith places value on people because we are God's creation, the object of his love, as shown in Ephesians.
5. Each one of us can be participating members of a community of faith, giving comfort to others as well as receiving comfort.

MASTER THIS: In order to conquer our anxieties, we need to become a part of a loving, caring community of Christian believers.

STUDY QUESTIONS

1. What are the characteristics of relationships that help us conquer fear?
2. What lesson about relationships do we learn from the story of Soeur Marie?
3. In the last four chapters we learned several important elements provided by the spiritual life

that are necessary for conquering fear. Review them.

4. Name the two interrelated issues addressed by interaction in the community of faith.

5. Being a part of the community of faith provides a

_____.

6. This puts relationships in the context of _____

_____.

7. Name the three most basic concerns in our society and show what kind of fear may spring from each.

8. Explain how our Western cultural value of competitive individualism contributes to our general sense of anxiety.

9. List the ways in which relationships in the community of faith can help us overcome anxiety as seen in Ephesians.

10. Give seven tips for helping others to deal with anxiety.

11. List the persons who make up your nurturing community of faith.

12. What can you do to develop open and loving interaction with this group of people?

9
CREATING A
CLIMATE OF CONFIDENCE

CHAPTER SUMMARY

In order to keep on conquering fear, our lives need an inner climate of confidence.

We must replace a spirit of timidity (cowardice) with confidence, as seen in 2 Timothy 1:7. Paul suggests three substitutes for timidity, all of which contribute to an inner climate of confidence:

1. Power—*dunamis* is the inexhaustible energy that comes from God.
2. Love—*agape* is the love that focuses on others rather than ourselves.
3. Self-discipline—*sophronismos* is self-discipline that draws upon moderation, good judgment, and prudence.

Fears may come unbidden, but we have the choice of what to do with them. Choose to take some practical steps to deal with fear.

1. React with thoughtfulness rather than emotion by asking the following questions:
    a. Do my emotions have a physical source in illness or exhaustion?
    b. Do my emotions reflect major issues that need to be resolved?
    c. Have traumatic and upsetting events taken place in my life immediately before these attacks of fear?

2. Employ one or more practical tools for breaking fear's grasp:
    a. wholesome and enjoyable activity
    b. relaxation through breathing exercises or imaging
    c. balancing the mental and physical input and output of life with periods of rest and relaxation

The way to maintain a climate of confidence in our lives is suggested in the roots of the word *confidence*: *fidere*, which means "to trust," and *con*, which means "with." Walking with God in a "together" trust is the way to maintain a climate of confidence as shown in Jeremiah 17:5–8.

The concluding story of the author's experience with the sailboat in Haiti illustrates this concept. Just as the sail maintains stability for the boat, our consistent walk with God in a "together" trust maintains an inner climate of confidence for us.

Chapter Study Guides

KEY THOUGHTS

1. In order to keep conquering fear, we need to maintain an inner climate of confidence.
2. We can replace timidity (cowardice), with power, love, and self-discipline. All are gifts from God as we walk with him. They are spiritual resources.
3. Our fears may come to us uninvited, but we can choose what to do with them by rationally thinking about them instead of reacting on an emotional level. Certain key questions may be asked.
4. We may employ activity, relaxation, or balance of mental and physical activities to conquer fear.
5. We can maintain an inner climate of confidence instead of fear by walking with God in a "together" trust relationship.

MASTER THIS: When fear sweeps over us, we can learn to manage it through thoughtful analysis and practical activity. We can maintain that inner climate of confidence through walking with God in a "together" trust relationship.

STUDY QUESTIONS

1. What do we need to keep on conquering fear?
2. What is the meaning of timidity as it is used in 1 Timothy 4:12?
3. List three character traits God gives us in place of timidity according to 2 Timothy 1:7, and describe each from the original words used by Paul.
4. What three questions can we ask about fear that will help us resolve it?
5. What three tools can we use to break fear's power over us?
6. What kind of activity should we employ to break fear's grasp?

7. Describe a relaxing "breathing" exercise that can help to break fear's grasp.

8. Explain what is meant by "imaging" and explain how it helps in managing fear.

9. How does balanced mental, physical, and emotional input and output help manage fear?

10. Define confidence according to its two root words.

11. How do we obtain confidence from our walk with God?

12. Do you need to establish a "together" trust relationship with God? If so, how will you do it? Psalm 20 offers suggestions.